The Essential Guide to...

BURNOUT

"*Our society has been slow to recognise how common burnout is and how damaging it can be, not just for the person affected but also for their family. In this excellent book, the Procters explain in non-technical language what burnout is, how to recognise that you have it (or are at risk of suffering from it), how to recover, and how to avoid a repetition. It contains much good advice, especially about the practical things that you can do to aid recovery, and a number of telling personal accounts that help to increase our understanding of how burnout happens and how it feels to suffer it.*"

Paul Britton, MIND

"*With a warm, considered approach and a blend of scientific and humanistic language this book has universal appeal. It is easy to read, enriched with case illustrations, and thoughtfully arranged with many helpful and original suggestions for preventing and managing burnout. I envisage this uplifting but realistic text being enormously beneficial for prevention, in addition to an essential guide for recovery. Whether it is you or somebody you know feeling the strain, the descriptions and explanations will enhance understa_____ t. I cannot praise th*

Dr Jean _____ onsultant
Child P_____

D1078445

Dedication

To our four children,
Kate, Emily, Will and Ed

The Essential Guide to...

BURNOUT

OVERCOMING EXCESS STRESS

*Andrew &
Dr Elizabeth Procter*

LION

Published by Lion Books
an imprint of
Lion Hudson plc
Wilkinson House, Jordan Hill Road,
Oxford OX2 8DR, England
www.lionhudson.com/lion

ISBN 978 0 7459 5585 8
e-ISBN 978 0 7459 5791 3

First edition 2013

Acknowledgments
pp. 25, 29–30: Extracts from *Jonny: My Autobiography* by Jonny Wilkinson,
copyright © 2011 Jonny Wilkinson, reproduced by permission of Headline
Publishing Group Limited.

A catalogue record for this book is available from the British Library

Printed and bound in the UK, September 2013, LH16

Contents

Acknowledgments

· ·

We especially wish to thank all those who were willing to share their personal story of stress and burnout with us. We are also very grateful to Helen Leach, Kate Mendez and Emily Wingfield for their help in typing and commenting on the script.

Introduction

· · · · · · · · · · · · · · · · · ·

This book is about burnout. Maybe you are reading it because you think you are heading that way, or because you know someone who is in that situation, or you may have been given the book because you have burnt out. Whatever your situation, we sincerely hope this book will be a tool in your full recovery, or help you support someone else.

If you are reading for your benefit, the fact that you have managed to get hold of it, open it and read these words shows that you have the motivation and energy to get better. This is great. It is the seed of your recovery. We hope that your reading of it will water and nurture that seed until it grows up into a full recovery.

Burnout is an official disorder. Once thought to be an illusion, it is recognized as a genuine diagnosis. It has a category in the latest International Classification of Diseases (ICD-10) as a "life management disorder".

Burnout is big. A recent survey estimates that one-third of British business workers will suffer from it at some stage in their careers. At any one time, half a million people are suffering from work-related stress that makes them ill. Work-related stress accounts for 10 per cent of the workforce being ill and off work. In the UK, 6.5 million working days per year are lost because of stress. This makes work-related stress the second largest category of occupational ill health in industry as a whole.

These are very frightening statistics. Behind every single one of them is a tragic personal story. For this book we have interviewed various people who have suffered from burnout, including Ed. This is the beginning of his story.

CASE HISTORY: ED

Ed is a tall man, and on the last day of a holiday in a villa in Italy with his wife and young family, he banged his head on one of the door lintels. It was not an unusual thing in itself; being so tall he was accustomed to banging his head. This time, however, the small incident proved too much for him. Without him realizing it, he was on the floor, curled up in a ball, weeping uncontrollably. His wife had to take over, drive the family to the airport and get them home.

Banging his head was the last straw in a long sequence of events leading to Ed burning out. He had been under prolonged stress through overwork. He had been promoted to the board of directors at his firm while still a relatively young man, and was under intense pressure to perform. "Work was pretty much all there was," he says. This led to him reassessing his values in life. He spent a lot of time talking things through with a number of people, and in the end chose to change jobs. He now has a very good job, but with a very different, healthier outlook on life. He has new priorities, especially about his family and other close relationships.

Ed's full story is given at the start of our first chapter.

ABOUT THE BOOK

This book explains how to recognize when we are burning out, understand what is happening, address what to do next and make a good and positive recovery. It is divided into three parts.

Part One is more factual. It explains what burnout is and how it works. It also gives measuring exercises to help assess how burnt out we are.

Part Two has three chapters on practical things to address when we are well down the road to burnout. They are written to help us in the immediate circumstances of burnout, and use the motif of the red, amber and green of traffic lights. The red chapter is about stopping, the amber chapter about waiting, getting ready to move forward, and the green chapter helps in thinking about the direction in which to go.

Part Three looks at many different facets of life. We emphasize that burnout need not be an end, but can be a beginning of a much more richly satisfying life, a much-needed opportunity to reconsider and remake life choices. This part addresses creativity, spirituality, relationships, getting to know and understand yourself, lifestyle, creativity and culture. It is designed to offer a wide choice of new opportunities in life as we recover.

The final chapter is on how to avoid burnout in the future. It offers a template for planning an ongoing lifestyle free from it.

Each chapter of the book answers a common question asked by people when they get into burnout. While we have tried to make the book progress from its beginning through to its end, please feel free to dip in and mix around the chapters, depending on your interests and requirements. Many of the chapters have suggested exercises. We recommend that you try as many of these as you can. Recovery depends on being able to do things rather than read about them, and it is in the doing of the exercises that the real road to recovery will begin.

This book is an introductory guide, written in non-technical language. It does not offer a deep analysis of emotional and mental health. It is designed to be easily understandable and to offer practical assistance. A final section gives suggestions for further reading and resources if you want to learn more. Where the exercises have suggested getting in touch with specific organizations, their contact details are listed there.

Interviews We have interspersed interviews throughout the book. We interviewed sixteen people in all, from all walks of life, and we are deeply grateful to each one of them. We have changed their names to protect their privacy, and placed one full interview at the start of most chapters. The interviewees' names and occupations are:

Clare, fifty-four, consultant psychiatrist
Richard, sixty-nine, a retired priest and writer
Justin, sixty-one, head teacher
John, sixty-two, a civil engineer and team skills training consultant
Sarah, fifty-two, editor
Suha, fifty-four, social worker
Beth, forty-four, family therapist
Ed, thirty-eight, company director
Ross, forty-six, multinational insurance company worker
Austin, thirty-six, art director
Michael, thirty-three, church minister
Heather, sixty, a teacher
Jane, fifty-five, secretary
Nicola, sixty, translator and interpreter
Margaret, forty, designer
Lily, sixty-one, advertising executive

There are snippets from the stories dotted through the text as well, to illustrate particular points. Some of these short illustrations are from others besides those sixteen people. We also draw on stories about people in the public eye.

OUR OWN STORY

We are not above the battle with burnout. We write from the experience of having grappled with it – and writing this book nearly burnt us out!

Andrew was involved in a serious car crash the week after signing the contract to write it. The following day he was offered a further major piece of work he had wanted to do for thirty years. A bit dazed, he accepted it. All this was on top of an existing busy life as a parish priest and part-time therapist. As time progressed, his stress levels grew and he got behind with all the work. He found himself sleeping badly, being overemotional, behaving intemperately at times and having an overall sense of detachment. He very nearly ground to a halt.

Elizabeth, as well as having to write the book and deal with her concern for Andrew, unexpectedly found her work situation revolutionized. A new Trust took over her department in NHS psychiatry. This meant a change of works practice and premises, a lot of uncertainty, and many delays and meetings. As a senior consultant she had to address this as well as deliver her own, already demanding, clinical workload.

These same months were happily busy for us in the family. We each had a landmark birthday, a new grandchild arrived and our son got engaged with consequent wedding plans to arrange.

It was hard to keep our heads above water. In fact we joked that when we had written the book we would buy it and do what it says to get out of our own burnout. In the end, Andrew took antidepressants for the first time and got some post-traumatic counselling. Elizabeth got by with a great many powerful statements that she was never, ever, ever going to write another book. And she hoped everybody got that.

TWO FINAL SUGGESTIONS

Before starting on the book properly, we suggest two things:

Find a comfortable place to read it. This could be a favourite armchair, the bath, Starbucks, a park bench, a favourite nook down at the local – anywhere that feels good. Or it could be a combination of places. Life will have been hard recently if reading this book is necessary, and a lot of what we say in it is about giving permission to enjoy life again. So a good start is to make the process of reading it a pleasure. Try reading while eating or drinking things you enjoy, so you look forward to exploring the next chapter. We hope this will enhance what we have to say, and build up a general hopefulness that life can and will improve from now on. The burnout is coming to an end.

Keep a journal. We regularly recommend using writing. Writing has lots of benefits. It cements our intentions and thoughts – makes them firmer and clearer – into a permanent form which can be referred to again. Not only is this useful in itself, keeping a journal can provide a companion on the way out of burnout. It can break up any loneliness and isolation, and is potentially a very powerful tool in recovery.

It's good to get an attractive notebook especially for this task, rather than just having random jottings on pieces of paper. You may prefer to work on a computer, perhaps doing a blog. In either case, it needs to be kept private.

PART ONE

· · · · · · · · · · · · · · · · · ·

This first part of the book is designed to help you understand how burnout works and assess whether you might be heading for it. We give guidance on the major symptoms of burnout, how stress works and can become overstress, and factors in life which tend towards burning us out.

I

What is Burnout and Have I Got It?

Here is the full version of Ed's story, of which we have seen a little already.

Interview: Ed

I was a company director in the manufacturing industry. Manufacturing is a dynamic industry with lots of excitement and constant decision-making. There is extreme pressure to deliver – it is not uncommon to have to work late and go in at weekends. It is a very male and macho world with lots of bravado, but also covering up.

I was a fast track career person. Work was pretty much me; I didn't have anything I could talk about outside of work. At the age of thirty-five I was with a new company and being given more responsibilities. I had a long commute each day, and at home all the domestic talk was about moving nearer to my work and finding more quality time to spend with my young family. That year we took a holiday in Italy. It was not the relaxing time I had hoped for and as a consequence I became frustrated, tired and angry. Toward[s] the end of the holiday I smacked my head on a low door lintel. I started to sob and sob. I curled up on the floor. I thought, "I can't go on any more" but I realized I had to go back to work almost more tired than when I started the vacation.

Once back in the UK, I continued to lose confidence in myself and went into a period of low mood and self-questioning. I suppressed it by working harder and managing to disguise the symptoms. No one at work was aware [of] how I was feeling. At home it was a different matter; I was impatient with my young children and getting more distant from my wife.

Following a restructuring of the business, I was overlooked for promotion and did not get on with my new boss. Overall the new job was unchallenging. I reconsidered my career and took voluntary redundancy. This led to a period of depression.

Through the support of my wife and close friends, I started to look at the alternative career options available and set about planning a new start that would combine work and home life in a more balanced way.

I attribute getting better to keeping a reflective diary, reading and understanding what was happening to me. I realized I was treating my wife and family as trappings of the success of my career. A friend suggested I try writing down what I thought was my purpose in life. I was surprised when it didn't mention work! I thought hard about what I wanted to be remembered for, beyond my job title and prestige. I tried to develop clear boundaries between home and work. I learned how to say no, to turn off my BlackBerry and give quality time to my wife and children.

I think individuals have to recognize themselves what is happening, and that all too often you don't recognize it until it is too late. Ask yourself if you have a supportive network around you, and whether you have empowered them to give you honest feedback. If you have, are you receptive to it? And try to get feedback from as many sources as are relevant.

Overall, I have gained from having taken the time and effort to really understand who I am and what I am like when at my best. I have made my life less chaotic and cluttered by saying no to some things; I try to engage fully in all aspects of my life. I am less ambitious and see life as not simply being work-focused.

....

Ed's case is a classic one of burnout through overwork. But what is burnout? This first chapter looks at what burnout is, and offers ways we can assess if we are suffering from it.

WHAT IS BURNOUT?

Burnout can be very difficult to define, even though it is so prevalent and we all think we know what we mean by it. Burnout doesn't happen to us overnight but is the end result of a long and often slow process described as:

> *being driven by an ideal, working harder and harder,*
> *putting one's own needs last, feeling miserable,*
> *isolated and denying what is happening, the death*
> *of one's values leading to cynicism, frustration and*
> *disengagement, feelings of inner emptiness and finally*
> *both physical and mental collapse.*[1]

The International Classification of Diseases (ICD-10) lists the following symptoms of burnout:

- physical and mental exhaustion and fatigue after minimal effort

- muscle aches and pains

- dizziness

- tension headaches

- sleep disturbance

- an inability to relax

- irritability

- inability to recover after rest, relaxation or entertainment.

All these symptoms need to last at least three months, and they should not be able to be explained by a different illness (such as depression). Is this true of you? Then maybe you are burnt out.

BURNOUT AND STRESS

Burnout comes when we overdo it for too long, and when our energy is used up faster than it is restored. "Burnout is not an event but the end point in burning down."[2] However we define burnout, we know that it is fundamentally about our levels of stress.

Stress is a normal part of our make-up. We use the word "stressed" when someone is not coping well, but doctors and psychologists talk about a "stress response" to mean a whole range of physiological changes that our brain triggers in order to prime our body to be alert and ready for action. "Stress" has become a catch-all term to describe the body's reaction to pressure (more on this in Chapter 3). But for now, what we need to know is that the body produces an array of hormones in response to a range of things, including danger, but also to normal life events, even meeting a friend. This response is designed to be a short-term reaction; the hormones are produced for specific events, and then their levels in the bloodstream die away. However, problems begin to occur if we are under prolonged pressure (chronic stress) and the stress hormone levels remain very high for a long period. This will mean they do not return to their normal resting state, but continue to be pumped round in the bloodstream. If they become a permanent feature of everyday life, we will eventually get burnt out.

Another writer on burnout, the psychiatrist Glenn Roberts, whose model we use later in this chapter, says, "Burnout is not the result of stress but of mismanaged stress."[3] You might like to think over the concept of chronic stress for yourself. Do you think you have pushed yourself beyond your natural limits for too long?

WHERE DOES BURNOUT COME FROM?

One way to see where the excess stress is coming from is to think about internal and external pressures.

External pressures

Burnout is often connected with professional work, and that is where most of the research has been done. Life at work can become so stressful that it takes over and eclipses all else. Studies show that when people feel torn between home and work, work usually wins. But stress within family circumstances, particularly among long-term carers, can prove to be too much. Burnout, however, need not be limited to one scenario. Overstress can result from different parts of our lives all going wrong together and, as we say, "It all begins to get too much." As more people, especially women, balance both a working life and a caring family role, this can lead to excess stress.

Jane had demands on her from work, her frail elderly mother, and her son and daughter, and at times she didn't know who to put first. It was only a matter of time before she began to feel unwell, and she described herself as "stressed". Her resources were overstretched and she pushed herself to the limit. She had no time or opportunity to relax, nor for her stress hormones to return to normal. They were constantly being pumped out to keep her going, and their normal ebb and flow had been lost. If Jane continued like this, she would inevitably suffer burnout.

Burnout can affect young people too. Margaret had her first episode of burnout when she was sixteen and pushing herself very hard for her GCSEs. She says, "I began to feel exhausted and had flu-like symptoms and was tearful. It took me nine months to recover."

Sometimes, something unforeseen triggers or compounds burnout. This can be something trivial, such as Ed banging his head in the villa in Italy. This small thing acted like the last straw breaking the camel's back. But sometimes a more serious traumatic incident can be a compounding factor. Dr Dina Glouberman mentions a person in her book, *The Joy of Burnout,* who was already under much work-related stress but whose burnout was compounded by a house fire.[4] The unforeseen event need not necessarily kick in immediately. I (Andrew) was involved in a car accident soon after agreeing to write this book. I then took on another major piece of work. But it was not till six months later that I began to have post-traumatic symptoms of nightmares, weeping fits, temper fits, feeling detached from everything. With the excess stress, I very nearly burnt out.

So burnout can be work-related, family-related, triggered by something out of the blue, or a mixture of these different elements.

Exercise
Consider your circumstances, and using a scale of 1 to 10, where 1 is "I don't feel under any stress at all in this area" and 10 is "I am under so much stress in this area I don't know if I can carry on", write down what your current scores are in the following areas:

- work

- family

- trigger event (something unexpected and difficult to deal with).

Having done this, go on to a composite measure, and consider all the areas of your life together on a scale of 0 to 10, where 0 is "Everything is fine. I could go on like this forever" and 10 is "I do not know if I can carry on like this much longer".

Having added up your scores, consider the answers. A score of 5 or over is worth noting, especially in the final, composite score. Such a score would mean taking a good look at stress levels and the pressures on you. It might also help to compare your scores with how you think you would have fared six months or a year ago. If you are feeling now that your stress levels have increased in that time, then it is even more vital to look closely at whether you are in danger of burnout.

Internal pressures

The pressures we have so far looked at are external, the demands of others: our boss, work colleagues, family, friends or unforeseen events. There are also inner pressures coming from our own expectations of ourselves. As we shall see more fully later, people who have high expectations of themselves are especially vulnerable to burnout. They drive themselves on, ignoring warnings, until they are constantly overstressed. This can be particularly true of professional sportspeople, whose self-esteem is linked to their athletic achievements, and who can suffer from a chronic lack of mental and physical recovery.

Exercise

To measure internal pressures, consider the following potentially true statements. Score them on a scale of 0 to 5, where 0 would be "This is not true of me at all" and 5 would be "Yes, that's me all over".

- I expect high standards of myself and those around me.

- When I have done a piece of work, I usually think it's rubbish and wish I'd done it better.

- I am prepared to sacrifice myself a lot to get an important task done.

- I really want to do something important in my life.

- I want to do a lot of good in the world before I die.

- When I plan a day, I aim to get far more done than I end up doing.

- I back my own judgment against that of most other people.

- I beat myself up a lot.

- When things go wrong, I tend to blame myself.

- If I'm honest, it would take a miracle for everything always to go as well I hope it will.

Any scores of three or above, for at least half of these questions, can be an indication of a lot of inner pressure, most of the time. The same would be true if the total score is 30 or over (the potential maximum score is 50).

Changes in our lives

Another measure of burnout can be looking at changes in us. Dr Glenn Roberts, whom we mentioned before, lists the warning signs and symptoms of burnout under four headings in this area:

- changes in behaviour

- changes in feelings

- changes in thinking

- changes in health.[5]

We are going to use this template to monitor our recent behaviour and attitudes. We ask some questions under each heading and add some examples from either well-known people or those who have told us their stories. We suggest working through them, at your own pace, ideally writing some conclusions down, to see how applicable they are to you.

Changes in behaviour

1. Working harder and longer but achieving less
Consider the following. In the last few months, have you

- been putting in longer hours

- worked at home more

- felt you were not keeping up with things at work as well as you would like

- taken longer to do tasks

- found it harder to keep a sense of proportion about your workload

- found yourself less satisfied with work outcomes

- clock-watched

- been late arriving – or leaving

- felt you were losing your creative or problem-solving abilities?

In an extract from his autobiography in an article in *The Times*, rugby player Jonny Wilkinson writes:

> *In my mind I have visualized a perfect outcome
> for every kick, but when my practice doesn't match
> that, I have to take it out on something… I treat
> the problem as I do my kicking – right, work it out
> and stay here working it out until you have done so.
> But by focusing so intensely, I just make it worse… I
> need an off switch and I don't have one. I want to go
> with the flow, chill and relax, let it go… but I just
> can't live like that.*

Later he describes coming to a complete stop and having to take stock of everything.[6]

Two of our interviewees found their behaviour was changing. Exhausted through hard work, Heather found that she was becoming less effective, despite working longer hours. Sarah, meanwhile, found she could not function at work as she was used to doing. "Everything felt foggy and exhausting," she says.

2. An inability to pursue recreational and recovery needs
Again, in the past few months have you:

- become so absorbed in work that you have cut down your social life

- picked up from those around you that you are becoming boring

- forgotten the last time you had a good evening out

- found it difficult to forget about work

- found your time off is not spent creatively, but just lazing around

- felt you have to cram the chores (shopping, cleaning, cooking) into too little space?

A recent study suggested that thinking about work during leisure time and getting less than six hours sleep a night are key factors in subsequent burnout. One interviewee, Richard, said he had withdrawn from friends because of being over-busy.

3. Using mood-altering drugs to help cope with the increased demand
In order to keep going under great pressure, have you done any of the following:

- increased the amount of caffeine or alcohol you drink

- started or increased usage of recreational drugs

- smoked more

- eaten more fast food or binged

- used Internet porn

- craved treats to lift your mood?

Geraint Anderson, author of *Cityboy*, worked in banking and wrote:

> *The great coping strategy in the City is alcohol. That is very good on a short-term basis. Unfortunately many don't see it as short term, and eventually alcohol becomes an issue in its own right (especially if you're foolish enough to add cocaine into the mix).*

Describing a colleague on the verge of burnout, he wrote: "He chain-smoked and couldn't sit still."[7]

Changes in feelings

When we are on the verge of burnout we feel different from normal. How many of the following have become true for you lately?

- I've lost my sense of humour.

- I feel resentful more of the time.

- I feel powerless to change things.

- I feel a failure.

- I feel guilty that things are not going well.

- I feel responsible all the time.

- I have been more irritable at work and at home.

- I have had flashes of anger.

- I have "lost it" with someone.

....

Interview: Richard

Richard had his first episode of burnout while a vicar in what was termed a "problem" parish. This coincided with him also doing a part-time job for his diocese and the birth of his third child. He says:

I simply ran out of steam due to overwork. I felt sudden and total physical weakness, was tearful and crying and had no appetite. Emotionally I felt isolated and cut off from everything and people, wrapped up in darkness, and I was very anxious because I did not know what was happening to me. Others told me later that I had been completely withdrawn and uncommunicative and very exhausting to be with.

....

Among our other interviewees, Clare felt anxious and was moody and angry, Beth was tearful and low in mood, and Suha often felt like crying and developed panic attacks related to driving. Heather was tearful and lost confidence, while Justin's family noticed he was short-tempered, tired all the time and intolerant.

Changes in thinking

As well as feeling different from normal, when we are on the edge of burnout we have changes in our thinking. How many of the following are true of you?

- I have had increasing thoughts about leaving my job.

- I have found it increasingly difficult to concentrate.

- I am more cautious and suspicious about things.

- I have become cynical and expect things to turn out badly.

- I have developed a victim mentality.

- I am preoccupied with my own needs and personal survival, and don't care about the bigger picture.

Margaret lost confidence and found even small challenges overwhelming. She was unable to handle situations she could normally deal with. She says, "You are running on past empty and the smallest thing makes you fall to pieces and burst into tears." Heather found she couldn't read or spend time on the computer, and Suha described feeling muddled and forgetful. Jonny Wilkinson wrote, "A sense of helplessness dominates my summer days. Everything seems pointless."[8]

Changes in health
Excess stress affects our health, causing physical problems, especially in wearing down our immune system. It is often linked to digestive and skin disorders, and insomnia. How many of the following are true of you?

- I have been getting frequent minor illnesses.

- I am more susceptible to coughs and colds.

- My sleep pattern is all over the place.

- I have had digestive problems.

- My skin has been a problem and I have had psoriasis.

- I have been more likely to burst into tears.

- I have started to worry about my mental health.

- I cry a lot and can't stop.

- I yo-yo: sometimes I'm fine and then suddenly I feel miserable.

- I feel tired all the time.

Jonny Wilkinson writes: "I am acutely aware of every kind of tiredness."[9]

Many of our interviewees had physical symptoms: Clare suffered from muscular pain and feeling exhausted, while Beth was exhausted and tearful. She also developed a sore throat, which led to a severe rash. Ross, meanwhile, had a throat infection during his annual leave, and on his return to work, discovered he could not function properly at all.

BURNOUT MEASURES

As we say in the Introduction, this book avoids being technical or overly scientific. It has been designed for the reader who is already at the end of their tether and who needs a simple approach. We trust that what we have supplied in this opening chapter is enough to help those who are worried about burnout to identify how realistic their fears are.

There are several more technical measures for burnout. The most famous is the Maslach Burnout Inventory, which measures exhaustion, cynicism and effectiveness. It is particularly focused on those who work with people in some capacity. The BMA has the Oldenburg Burnout Inventory on its website, a questionnaire with sixteen questions relating to energy levels and attitude, available for doctors to assess their level of burnout. There are many others to be found online. We give the details for these measures, plus those for some other more general stress measures, in the Resources section at the end of the book. It may be that some readers want to use them in addition to what we have put in this chapter. You probably have a good idea of whether you are close to burnout or are already there, but it can be helpful to see it in black and white.

2

Brownout or Burnout?

Sometimes we can wonder if we are approaching burnout, but feel that we are not there yet. After all, we are holding everything together – just – even if we have worrying symptoms (maybe many of those listed in the last chapter). We have not collapsed completely and have been able to carry on. So, if that is you, you may have what is termed "brownout".

WHAT DO WE MEAN BY BROWNOUT?

Brownout is the stage before burnout, when we

- have felt overstressed and pressurized for some time, and it is beginning to take its toll on us physically and emotionally

- notice changes in our behaviour, feelings, thinking and health

- are near to being physically and emotionally exhausted to the point of collapse

- hang in there by the skin of our teeth

- have lost our idealism, and our energy is gone.

Kate Middleton, in her book *Stress: How to De-stress Without Doing Less,* uses the term "presenteeism", describing when we are at work but not working effectively because of stress.[1]

Perhaps we have dependants and this drives us to keep on going. Even if there aren't any people depending on us to be in work, we have our pride and we don't want to look a loser in front of our colleagues and friends. And we don't want to disappoint ourselves either, given that we began our careers with such high hopes. It may be difficult to think of what else we can do, anyway. So we continue to function, but in our heart of hearts we are exhausted and there is no savour left in what we do. This is brownout.

If we think of burnout and well-being as opposite ends of a sliding scale, brownout is very near the burnout end, but not quite there. To illustrate this, let us look at some case studies of people who have reached the point of brownout and pulled back from burnout.

....

Interview: John, part one

John's first episode of brownout occurred when he was in his twenties, when he was very busy and over-committed both in his home and work life, and also within the local community and church.

I began to feel extremely stressed and couldn't think straight. I knew I was not really managing the task I was currently working on, but I was constantly worrying about what I had to do next. I felt overloaded and had no "downtime" between the things I felt I had to do. I went to see my GP and was offered medication, but didn't want to take it, and simply kept going.

My wife got very worried about me and in the end compiled a diary of all I was doing, and made me sit and discuss it. Together we decided what I should pull out of and stop doing in order to recover, and in this way I slowly got better. I learned then that I had limits and tried to achieve a more sensible life balance.

....

Interview: Justin

Justin was a secondary school teacher. When he was thirty-five years old, he was appointed deputy head teacher in a very different type of school to his previous one. He says:

The new post was very different from what I expected. The school was very different and I replaced an acting post holder who was still in the school and unhelpful. I was given some very stressful responsibilities early in the post, and had to identify eight staff for redundancy. The head teacher was also under significant pressure and had a limited understanding of what I was experiencing. He was not very supportive. I developed poor sleep patterns; my sleep was often disrupted. I had some loss of appetite and persistent low level anxiety. I found I was unable to switch off work and relax at weekends and even in the school holidays. At night I would go to sleep but then wake suddenly with my heart racing, thinking about school issues. My family noticed I was short-tempered and tired all the time, and was intolerant.

I realized I was suffering from stress. I was able to talk to my wife, but it was a difficult time for her as well. I shared this with my twin brother, who listened well, but I didn't tell many others. I had to find my own solutions to the problem and I did some research into stress management. I planned positive activities [such as] holidays to look forward to, and worked hard at keeping issues in perspective. When I was unable to sleep I listened to music or read light books, and I became more sanguine about lack of sleep. Without strategies like these I would have ended up with burnout. Over time I got the measure of the job and found it less stressful, and my stress symptoms reduced. This experience has made me more self-aware and less ambitious. My priorities changed. I became more philosophical about my work. I survived in the post and went on to become a head teacher.

Interview: Sarah

Sarah had a temporary contract in her field of work. She says:

When I was fifty-one, as well as the uncertainty about my work, there were many external family pressures. My husband was applying for voluntary redundancy, one son was seeking to change careers, another son got married and my daughter was struggling at university. I felt very odd and went in on myself. Everything felt foggy and I had no energy, no enthusiasm nor ideas, which are crucial in my job. I began to get a lot of colds. I couldn't sleep and I felt as if I had masses of adrenalin onboard. I would think of something to do, such as hanging out the washing, and suddenly I would be awash with adrenalin. When that calmed down I would go into a supremely tired mode, like a zombie. Happy things made me cry and sad things didn't. I felt cut off from myself and couldn't face even small crises. I felt I had exhausted everything and I couldn't cope with people. My husband noticed the silence, and that I had gone off seeing people and meeting new people, which is not like me at all.

I didn't take time off work, as I was afraid of the backlog that would be waiting for me on my return. My work colleagues were very supportive but my immediate boss told me to get myself sorted out. I told my children just that I did not feel in a good place, and I was selective about which friends I spoke to, though most of them were very supportive. I did see my GP but I refused to take antidepressants, and somehow the symptoms just wore off. My job situation is still not resolved but I've stopped worrying about absolutely everything.

I think burnout is a process, a continuum that you can move up and down. Looking back, I wonder if I was truly burnt out or rather browned out, but I was displaying a lot of symptoms for quite a while and I reckon I came pretty near to burnout.

Interview: Clare

Clare is a recently retired consultant psychiatrist.

Ten years ago, I had a car accident which left me badly shaken and bruised and with whiplash. Despite recovering physically, I found it difficult to build back up to a busy work pattern. I had been working for a couple of years almost single-handed, with a very large and demanding caseload, prior to the accident. At home I had a hectic and busy lifestyle with four children all at different stages. Normally I have immense energy, but sometimes after the accident I found myself feeling exhausted, and started having lots of muscle pains. I felt very anxious about all sorts of things that previously hadn't bothered me, and others told me I was moody and angry.

At work I went to see the occupational health team who recommended that I worked a part-time timetable. Over some months I gradually built up my working hours until I could work full-time again.

Interview: Lily

Lily was three years short of retirement. She had worked for many years reasonably happily, handling advertising for a commercial journal. Then things changed. She says:

Two new bosses were appointed – my immediate boss, a female, and a new, male editor. Both of these quickly lost my respect by bringing in sweeping changes to work practice, in my view ineffectively. I began to hate the thought of going in to work, but I was unemployable elsewhere, and needed my full pension. I had the care [of] my infirm, elderly mother when not at work. We lived in the old family house, which was now too big and impractical. Between my job, my mother and the house, I felt totally worn down by life. I entered therapy. With the therapist's help, I devised strategies for survival until retirement. At work

I took my lunch hours, avoided confrontation and started a personal journal. At home I blocked in two to three hours for myself, arranging alternative care for my mother where possible. I began to look at possibilities for a smaller house. This, together with work on my self-worth, saw me through to retirement. I never liked the job but I survived.

....

John, Justin, Clare, Sarah and Lily were well on the way to burnout but fell short of needing to stop functioning in their roles. Anyone who is "browned out" would do well to include themselves among those for whom this book is written. Most of our remedies for burnout apply equally to brownout. Where they do not, we try to give specific extra advice applicable to brownout.

So, brownout people – please read on!

3

How Does Stress Affect Us?

· ·

Interview: Jane

Jane was a middle-aged woman working as a secretary when out of the blue her partner was made redundant. She is an example of how stress can pile up. She writes:

I felt the pressure of having to maintain my job to keep the mortgage payments going, but I coped reasonably well. Then my elderly mother fell and broke her hip, and needed time in hospital. I was very worried about her, but once she began to recover, I relaxed a little. Then when my mother was discharged back home, she needed a lot of extra support with the ordinary, everyday things of life. I wanted to do this for her and managed by cutting out some of my own leisure time, and pushed myself a bit harder. I visited my mum before work, did all her shopping and washing, and cooked a meal each night and took it round to her. It was hard going, and I felt more tired.

Then my son had a sports accident and was rushed into hospital needing urgent surgery. I didn't know whether to go to work, go to see my mother or go to my son's bedside. I felt I was needed in all three places at once, and I ended up rushing from one thing to another, without any time to relax or unwind. My son's operation went straightforwardly, but on the very day he was sent home from hospital, my daughter rang up in a panic complaining of chest pain. I rushed with her to Accident and Emergency, and I was up all night with her.

· ·

STRESSORS

Burnout follows prolonged times of stress. This chapter is about what happens to our bodies when we are stressed, and we may find that understanding and appreciating the effect of stress on our bodies will help us understand what has happened to us in burning out.

To be alive is to experience physical and emotional stressors on a regular basis. Our bodies and minds normally adapt to the different demands that daily life makes upon us. Stress responses

- are normal and integral to life

- can be physical or psychological

- are important for healthy bodies and minds

- can be caused by both pleasant and unpleasant things

- need to be linked to rest and recuperation.

Without stress, our bodies become weak and unhealthy. Exercise is very good for us, and yet it produces stress to our bodies. Walking is a form of exercise that involves the muscles putting strain and tension on the bones as they move. This in turn makes the bones stronger and increases the bone density, so that they do not become brittle and fracture easily. It is only when there is too much stress that it can cause damage.

There was a recent snippet in the press about a marathon runner who had noticed some pain in his hip during training. He kept on running, and had started to run the London Marathon when he felt the pain get much worse. However, he kept going and managed to complete the marathon, though limping all the way. Afterwards he was still in a lot of pain, and he had an X-ray of his hip. He had suffered a *stress* fracture to the neck of his femur (the bit where the thigh bone links to the hip), and needed an operation. The repeated stress on his hip through running had strained it so much that the bone had cracked.

Many things stress us physically, such as driving a car, getting a cold, or even eating a big meal. These are all part and parcel of daily life, and do not usually produce damage. As well as physical strain, mental and emotional strains also contribute to stress. Things that distress us and upset us are stressful, but so too are good things, such as falling in love, going on holiday or a big party celebration.

STRESS HORMONES: WHAT HAPPENS WITHIN?

When we find ourselves in a situation (or anticipate one) where we need to react or be ready for something, our body chemicals change. Part of our innate, autonomic nervous system, the sympathetic system, kicks into action unconsciously. It works to make our bodies and minds more efficient, and causes the release of several hormones into the blood (adrenaline, cortisol and noradrenaline), setting off a chain of chemical reactions. These hormones travel round in the blood and affect all parts of the body, preparing them for action. Glucose sugar is released into the bloodstream to provide energy for the muscles to use, the heart starts to beat faster, and breathing quickens to enable oxygen to be delivered to the brain and muscles. Blood is diverted from the skin and digestive organs to the muscles, and they tense, ready for action, and the pupils dilate so we can see more clearly.

This whole process is often known as the "flight or fight response", when the systems in the body are activated in order to enable us to perform at our peak, and it is inbuilt into our bodies. It can be very helpful in dangerous situations. If we are walking in a field and see a bull in the far corner, the system swings into action automatically, as soon as danger is perceived, enabling us to sprint to the fence and get out of danger. We don't need to consciously think about it and decide to run – we simply run. Afterwards we feel drained as the hormones ebb away, but relieved that we are safe. Our hormone levels will then return to normal as we rest and relax.

This same reaction happens in a quieter way every time we are faced with a perceived demand, be it driving in heavy traffic, giving a presentation at work, or having a disagreement with a loved one. Chemicals are automatically released to prepare us for action and these chemicals prepare our bodies to work more efficiently.

PERFORMANCE AND STRESS

People's general performance improves with the increased arousal produced by stress hormones, up to an optimum point. With too little stress we are bored and under-perform. Moderate amounts of stress are stimulating and enable us to perform well. If the stress continues to increase above this level, or is chronic and ongoing in nature, we become exhausted, feel fatigued and our performance rapidly deteriorates to the point of breakdown. This is called the inverted "U" curve.[1] Although when we are under stress we fully intend to push ourselves harder as the stress increases further, the reality is that our performance actually declines, and eventually, if there is no reduction in the level of stress, we become ill and break down, and are unable to function normally.

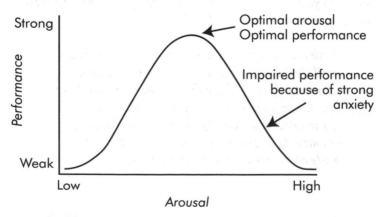

THE NEED FOR RECOVERY

Serious problems with stress begin when the normal ebb and flow of stress hormones is disrupted. This can happen when one demand after another is thrust upon us and we do not have the time or opportunity to rest properly in between them. Without time to unwind and relax, we never get back to our normal resting state, and we begin to live in a state of ongoing arousal, with high levels of stress hormones circulating in our blood. The effect of these hormones is to make us feel tense and shaky, look pale, have muscle aches and pains and tension headaches. Our concentration will be poor, and we will sleep badly. We may end up going to see our GP with a variety of physical complaints that are really caused by the prolonged effects of stress hormones on our body.

A persistent high level of the stress hormone cortisol eventually causes a depletion of the circulating steroids in the blood. These steroids maintain our energy levels and our ability to resist stress. When stress is constant and chronic, even the body's store of cortisol becomes empty. Then our energy and immunity reduce and we become very susceptible to viruses and feel fatigued. If nothing is done, this ultimately leads to complete exhaustion.

Bette Midler, the American actress, suffered adrenal exhaustion after two years in Las Vegas with her *Showgirl Must Go On* show, and said in an interview in *The Times*:

> *Work has always been how I feed myself creatively*
> *until the last couple of years. I just got exhausted,*
> *burnt myself out. Physically I didn't have anything*
> *left. The obligation was to keep going whether*
> *you wanted to or not. By the end I was having a*
> *vitamin B12 shot every night. I was whipped; I*
> *really didn't know who I was anymore.*

> *I couldn't play music, couldn't listen to music,*
> *and couldn't do anything. I wasn't having a nervous*
> *breakdown. I had a little bit of a collapse, lay*
> *down, and puttered around in my pyjamas all day.*
> *Eventually I started talking to a therapist, working*
> *out again, picked up a guitar.*[2]

She now feels much better but did not feel able to take on a couple of Broadway roles she was offered, recognizing that eight shows a week would be too much.

ONE MAN'S STRESS...

When we consider optimal stress levels and not being overstressed, we need to remember that we are all made very differently. What may seem like intolerable stress to one person is the level of stress that results in another's best performance. Why should this be?

The perceived demands on us

Our perception of situations affects how we feel about them. The way we think about potentially stressful demands affects our stress levels. We will be asking ourselves the following questions:

- Is this going to take a lot of time and effort?

- Can I actually cope with that right now?

- Will it matter if I say I can't do it?

How we answer these questions will affect how stressed we feel.

So if we are asked to take on an extra job, and it is something that we have done before and are familiar with, we won't feel as stressed as we would if it were totally new. We might even relish the challenge and think it could be fun. However, if we feel we barely have time to do all that is expected of us anyway, an extra task might seem like the last straw, and massively increase the sense of stress and pressure on us. We could refuse to do it, but if our new boss has asked us, it will be important to us to appear in a good light. We might be asked by someone we love who is in need, such as an elderly relative, and we agree to take on more despite our misgivings. In this case, the task will feel demanding, we will wonder if we can cope and yet we will feel we must do it and not let people down. This will be very stressful.

Our underlying personality and temperament

Some of us are born with a very relaxed and laid-back temperament. Little seems to bother us. Others find challenges and deadlines stimulating, and work best doing things at the last minute under pressure. If we are more emotionally reactive to situations and quickly feel anxious and stressed, we may find it difficult to tolerate even moderate stress – so it is very important to *both understand and know ourselves*, and to accept the way we are and learn to accommodate that as much as we are able.

Anticipation

Anticipation affects our stress levels. Often if we are bored we think about some enjoyable future situation, such as meeting a good friend, and as we anticipate it, we feel excited and interested. However, we also anticipate difficult demands on us, such as driving a long way or having to give a speech, or keeping going without a holiday. The very act of anticipation actually raises our stress hormone levels. We all feel nervous (and stressed) at the prospect of something different or something we perceive as difficult. If, for instance, a loved one has to have a major operation, we may be very stressed ourselves as we anticipate what might go wrong.

Uncertainty and lack of control

Uncertain situations are usually more stressful than those we know something about, as are circumstances outside of our control. We become less stressed when we have had training for situations at work (speaking to an audience, doing a new job) and when we have some control and input into the situation. If we are expected to do things at work for which we have had no training, and become severely stressed, we may become ill as a result.

In 1997, a Post Office worker suffered a breakdown as a result of overwork and lack of training on new systems. When he returned to work after four months off sick, his managers promised flexible working arrangements to allow him to gradually take on his normal workload. However, they failed to implement them, with the result that he became severely stressed and had to go off sick again. He was able to bring a successful claim in the High Court against his managers.[3]

HOW DO WE KNOW WHEN WE ARE OVERSTRESSED?

Usually we feel overtired by stress once we get beyond our optimal stress levels, but we may need to push ourselves on regardless, and so begin to experience other symptoms. We have written more fully about this in Chapter 1, so just briefly mention them again.

Physical symptoms

These might include:

- muscle pain

- headaches

- poor sleep

- digestive problems.

Psychological symptoms

Too much stress can mean we:

- cannot concentrate

- become forgetful

- struggle to make decisions

- take on too much

- have poor judgment

- suffer anxiety and panic attacks

- feel miserable or depressed.

As we shall see in Chapter 4, Suha, a social worker, experienced both physical and psychological symptoms when her increasing workload coincided with going through the menopause. She found sleep difficult, started to experience panic attacks, felt weepy and was muddled in her thinking.

She went to her GP complaining about the physical symptoms, but was advised to take time off work for stress, and when she did, her symptoms slowly improved.

STRESS SCALE

The most commonly used measure of stress levels is the Holmes and Rahe Stress Scale.[4] This is a questionnaire with forty-three life events outlined. Each life event is given a score, and those completing the questionnaire are asked to tick those they have experienced in the past year. So, for instance, Christmas is given a score of 12, getting married 50, and death of a spouse 100. After completing the questionnaire, the score is added up and then a stress rating is given. (This Stress Scale is widely available to do online and we mention how to access it in the Resources section.)

4

Are Some People More Vulnerable to Burnout Than Others?

Although people in all walks of life can experience burnout, the research work carried out on the condition suggests that professional people are more vulnerable to it, and especially those who are in the caring professions. Many unseen carers are also close to burnout, as we have seen with Jane.

Burnout is linked to two types of personality, both with the kind of qualities professional people are expected to show. Both of these have admirable elements but, as we shall see, if they are not balanced with other things, they can lead to burnout. The two types of personality are:

- people who are conscientious, hard-working, and highly motivated with drive and commitment

- people with high levels of compassion and concern for others, who have high ideals and are willing to sacrifice self in order to help others.

What can be wrong with these? Let's take them each in turn and see how they can lead to a vulnerability to burnout.

HARD-WORKING, CONSCIENTIOUS, HIGHLY MOTIVATED PEOPLE WITH DRIVE AND COMMITMENT

Donna Andronicos in her book *Coping with Burnout* says, "Passionate people who love their work are at high risk of burnout."[1] Burning bright and burning out are two potential consequences for competitive athletes driven by passion. People with these characteristics tend to rise to the top of their professions, and are given more and more responsibilities. They quite easily and quickly find themselves overburdened. Because they have dedication, they are prepared to make great sacrifices in order to see a high standard of achievement in their work. They expect high standards of themselves. Under the pressure that success brings, they can soon find themselves working exceptionally long hours.

They are sometimes categorized as "Type A" personalities, according to work originally done in the 1950s about stress levels and the incidence of heart disease. Type As are competitive, work-driven controllers. They want to dominate. They drive against deadlines. They don't relax easily. According to James Scala, "At social gatherings, they will not only turn the conversation around to a topic they want, they will dominate it as well. Or they will eavesdrop, slowly inject themselves into a conversation and then dominate it."[2]

They are often perfectionists, unable to relax unless everything is just right. Under the pressure of a heavy workload, and their own and other people's fallibility, mistakes creep in. People with this kind of personality can't brush these aside, but start to put in still more hours to get things up to standard. Because they are conscientious people, they have a tendency to blame themselves when things go wrong. They take mistakes to heart and assume everything is their own fault. Again, this drives them to get it put right and work ever harder at the expense of their time and energy.

Over time, under the pressure of all the hard work, a sense of proportion gets lost. Somehow, instead of trying to draw a line under all the work, the person becomes more unable to say no. They begin to take on even more, ignoring an inner sense of panic. They have to cover up that they are not coping and keep up an appearance of the old competence while actually they have started to not sleep properly. They no longer have a good diet and find they are suffering from all kinds of odd aches and pains.

They may need to keep going because they and others are dependent on their earnings, and they are unable to afford to take time off and slow down. This type of person sometimes has a deep insecurity, which means that not only must they do a good job but also must be seen to do so. Because they need to feel valued by working hard and succeeding, they bury these worrying signs and struggle on as best they can. They are strong people and can do this for quite some time. Then comes the crash. A morning arrives when they can't face work and they stay in bed, unable to get up. An incident happens when they completely lose it – bursting into tears or getting unacceptably angry. A spouse who has likely been sorely neglected during all this starts divorce proceedings.

The person implodes. Depression kicks in. They may become suicidal. They have to go off sick long term. This may cost them the very job for which they sacrificed so much.

....

Interview: Ross, part one

I had worked for a multinational insurance company for twenty or so years. My work involved a lot of overseas travel to Africa and Australia, and long, long hours when in the UK. When I first joined the firm, there was a pastoral, caring approach to the workforce, but this had disappeared, driven out by rising costs. The company was looking for profit and value from their workers and what profit they made was measured quarterly. The work environment pushed people to the maximum limits possible. Even taking annual leave was a struggle, as you were perceived as letting the team down if you took two weeks off.

When I was forty-two I had a bout of pneumonia, possibly as a result of overseas travel. I went back to work but never felt entirely well. Three to four years later, there was a period of intense travel… I would routinely be expected to fly to Australia, go straight into a daylong business meeting without sleep, and then fly back. Then I was transferred to work in Nigeria, where I found the corruption amongst work colleagues very depressing. I would regularly leave the house before six in the morning and not get back till nine at night. At home there was an exciting possible house move to a "dream home", which was emotionally consuming. At the same time I was troubled by my parents' divorce.

When I found myself not doing simple tasks well at work I didn't go to my GP, as to take any sick leave would have meant loss of face. I was increasingly tired and depressed. It reached a point where I could no longer take my regular jogs or play cricket for my local team, my sole recreation. I became tearful and my body ached all the time. I struggled on until my annual leave was due, and then spent the two weeks ill with a throat infection. On my return to work I found I couldn't function at all, had to go to the doctor and was given a month's sick leave. A series of tests uncovered an underlying disorder.

I had no support from my company when I went off sick, their reaction being to… prepare someone to step into my shoes [and then dismiss me]. After a threatened tribunal, my company gave me "gardening leave". My colleagues, I felt, would have been supportive but were all watching their own backs, and were aware that the management's view was "You are only as good as your last deal, which was today".

This is not the end of Ross's story. We hear more from him later.

PEOPLE WITH HIGH LEVELS OF COMPASSION AND HIGH IDEALS

There is an even stronger tendency to burnout among those in the caring professions than among those in industry or commerce. Again, this can be traced to the way in which the strengths of people who enter the caring professions and do well in them can cover weaknesses, which leads them to eventually burn out. This does not only apply to people who care professionally, but also to anyone who is in a caring role, paid or unpaid.

Obviously those who become doctors, nurses, psychologists, social workers, teachers, pastors and so on, do so because they care about people and want to make a change for the better in their lives. Highly dedicated, these professionals are prepared to undergo years of training and then work very hard in their caring roles. They are as susceptible to the vulnerabilities of high achievement as others are but, working with needy people, there are further weaknesses and dangers that can lead to burnout.

Ken Powell writes:

> *In the caring professions, the balance between a detached professional and a caring human being is a difficult one. Many who have become too involved and empathise by suffering with patients, find the pain and sorrow too much to bear... This is when "depersonalisation" takes over. We operate without feelings. Patients and clients are almost objects to us. We feel dead inside.[3]*

If helping people is our principal aim, we will have less tangible goals than those in business or commerce. It is not easy to measure whether we are being successful. How does the teacher know that their pupils are improving? How does the minister know their congregation's spiritual life is developing? How does the nurse know if they are caring well for their patients? In some cases, it might be possible to look at some facts and figures, but for most practitioners, people's needs are too complex and untidy for it to be easy to know how well they are doing.

People's needs are endless and there can be a sense of trying to empty the sea in one's work as a caring professional. People in need transfer their needs onto their carers in a profound psychological way that has been well researched and understood in the world of therapy. This leaves the carer, in a way, psychologically impregnated with the complex needs of the people they are caring for. Given that they are likely to be caring for large numbers of people, whether it is in a school, hospital or church, this becomes very emotionally draining. It becomes hard for the carer to switch off from their role precisely because they are compassionate and want to take on problems. They can become lost in the sea of need that they confront.

Those in the caring professions can also struggle because of the expectations placed on them by those they are looking after. The minister is expected to be a perfect paragon of Christian virtue. The nurse is expected to be always available and tender-hearted. The social worker is expected to be alert to people in need, often in very sordid circumstances, all the time. Teachers are often given a parental persona by their pupils and indeed by the pupils' parents. The dedicated, caring professional half believes this persona and tries to live up to it. Inwardly they half believe that they can be the ultimate solution to people's needs, but they also know that they are human and fallible and have a dark side. This creates a deep inner tension.

Over time, this can lead to a dangerous polarization of the caring professional's life. They have an outward life of care, concern and doing good. Yet inwardly they can become prone to despair, to addictive behaviours with drink, pornography or overeating. They can start to "take out" their troubles with the people they care for or on those close to them – their families, children and friends – by being erratic, bad-tempered and unpredictable.

The modern pressures on professional carers have racked up in recent years. In his book *Beyond Burnout* Cary Cherniss points out how in a recent survey the public's expectations of a good nurse had changed from "responsible, orderly, neat, prudent, industrious and sensible" to "empathic, giving, in tune with the emotional needs of their patients." He goes on to say, "Standards for caring and compassion have risen. We expect more of caring professionals than ever before."[4]

The highly motivated person in the caring profession is often disillusioned. They feel torn between what is expected of them by the system in which they work and the people for whom they care. Cynicism can come in, which is distressing to someone who has high ideals of helping others. Here is the story of a social worker:

....

Interview: Suha

Suha became unwell at the age of fifty-four. She says:

I had been a social worker for many years, and was very committed to the young people I worked with. I often had to work extra hours to fit everything in. I also [offered] a lot of support to my own children and grandchildren.

Around this time the administrative, clerical and secretarial support at work was lost, owing to retirements and cost-cutting measures. My secretary had always been very supportive and helpful, and losing her meant that I had to do many things for myself, [such as] phone calls and letters. At the same time as my already heavy caseload at work increased, I began to notice some menopausal symptoms.

I found myself unable to sleep because I was thinking constantly about what needed to be done at work. Out of the blue, I started to experience panic attacks connected to driving (an essential in my job – I visited many young people in their homes and frequently drove to meetings). My thinking was muddled and forgetful; I felt tired all the time and was weepy. My family told me that I was unable to sit and relax at all and that I always looked pale and tired.

My doctor signed me off work. I used medication to help with my pattern of sleep, and to reduce my high levels of anxiety. My family [was] very concerned about me, and they encouraged me to take more time to relax and to change my job if necessary. I felt I had a lot of support from my line manager and colleagues at work, and my friends who worked for Social Services gave me emotional support and understanding. I began to appreciate how I had contributed to reaching the point of burnout, and that I could go forward and recover.

I came back to my job recognizing that I needed to be more realistic about the amount of work I could do. I decided to plan breaks and to take back time I was owed for working over my paid hours. I knew that I needed to be more in tune with myself. Looking back, I can see what a bad place I was in.

STRENGTHS AND WEAKNESSES

Ross is an example of a high achiever in business who wasn't able to read the signals of burnout until it was upon him and he lost his job. Suha is an example of a person in the caring professions who needed time off work but was able to carry on in her profession. Both were victims of their own success. Both were fine people who burnt out, having started from a position of great commitment and achievement. It is ironic that these things are the leading causes of burnout. As is often the way in life, our strengths are bound up in our weaknesses and vice versa. The key to avoiding burnout is a proper balance in life between our work and our other relationships and activities, and a further balance between our strengths and weaknesses. We will look at ways to achieve this in the following chapters in this book.

What Other Factors
·····································
Contribute to Burnout?
·····································

Interview: John, part two

John is a retired civil engineer and a team skills training consultant. He has had two episodes of brownout/burnout over his working life. The first episode we mentioned in Chapter 2, when he was in his twenties. By the time he was in his mid-fifties, John was in a senior position at work with a team of twenty under him. He says:

The work was pressurized and I had too much to do. I felt it was never completed; there was the tyranny of unending emails and I had little satisfaction in my job. This was made worse by a change in senior management, and the reduction of the typing pool so that I had to do more administration myself. I felt squeezed between the senior manager and my team, and had to communicate policies I felt unhappy and sceptical about. The values of the manager mismatched my own values. I did not feel listened to by management and lost any sense of control in my work.

At home there were added pressures as my daughters reached their teenage years. I was working away from home from Monday to Friday each week, and after sixteen years of this I found the travelling tiring. I felt I needed to be a very present father at weekends. Life lost its savour and I became depressed, physically exhausted and found I couldn't sleep for long. I went to my GP and began to take antidepressants but they simply made me feel numb. I felt I oscillated between brownout and burnout but somehow I kept going.

One day, after I had been up until 3 a.m. producing information for a work meeting, I felt very anxious, over-focused on the task to the point where I had lost interest in anything else, and lightheaded. I had a sense of unreality, which cushioned the daily round. I realized I was not well and spoke to my boss, who referred me to a stress counsellor. She was very helpful and advised me to drink plenty of water; keep a notebook by my bed to jot down thoughts that were keeping me awake; take regular exercise – so I went swimming and attended the gym each week; buy a season ticket to attend rugby matches at weekends (I found the shouting for my team very cathartic and therapeutic as a means to reduce stress); cook for myself rather than [buy] ready meals. She also advised me to take time chopping vegetables, which I found reduced stress.

With these measures I managed to keep working, but my wife said I was constantly tired, complained regularly about my work situation but seemed unable to change it. I had a lot of insight into my problems and understood my strengths and weaknesses. My team skills analysis training had helped me to know and understand myself. I thought into things and discussed options with friends and listened to them as they reflected back to me.

I had always felt that my belief in something bigger and outside of myself gave my life meaning. My wife encouraged me to think about what I really wanted to do in my life, and with her encouragement I resigned from my job and enrolled to do a course at Bible college. The change in direction was liberating and energizing and gave me space to recover. After the year's course, I took on freelance consultancy work.

EXTERNAL FACTORS

In this chapter we will look at external factors that can have a profound effect on stress levels for individuals and lead to burnout. These are:

- **educational** factors and the expectations we have about ourselves and the workplace

- **occupational** factors and the effect of inadequate resources, management styles and long working hours.

EDUCATIONAL FACTORS

The preparation for many careers can be very theoretical, looking at problems and issues in an idealistic rather than a realistic way. So the trainee teacher, social worker, medical practitioner or business graduate has a lot of theoretical knowledge. Little is taught about the day-to-day reality of living the job and the inevitable frustrations of working with children who don't want to learn, deprived people, patients who fail to engage with treatments, or the realities of business life. Frustrations and disillusionments arise when we get into our daily job, especially when the first flush of idealism has worn off. Job satisfaction is reduced and this has been shown to contribute to burnout. We have probably not been trained to look after ourselves, or to cope with the stress of the job. Often, feeling stressed is still regarded as a weakness, and we can feel ashamed of admitting our struggles and vulnerabilities to others.

There are signs that this is changing. In certain fields, people are encouraged to have mentors or to join a peer support group. Some theological colleges and some medical and nursing schools include courses on understanding oneself and how to manage stress, but this is far from the norm. Resilience training has been suggested for social workers and counsellors to help them have more realistic expectations of themselves and their job role. There is inadequate training in managing psychosocial stress for nurses, and yet studies have shown that mentoring and guidance in effective stress management is essential to prevent future burnout.

But this does not address the problem of being ashamed of feeling under stress. It would be far better to have some inbuilt preparation and education in the training courses on how to look after oneself. In our opinion, it would be even better if school-age pupils were to start learning about stress and how to handle it, so that it would be seen as a normal part of life.

OCCUPATIONAL FACTORS

As well as education and preparation for work, what about the workplace itself? Ken Powell in his book *Burnout* says, "Organisations do not exist to be friendly or nice. They exist to fulfil a mission. Their mission may be clear or vague, obvious or covert; sometimes what is stated is very different in practice."[1]

Have changes in works organizations created a greater likelihood of burnout? We think that is highly likely. There are four main factors within work culture that contribute to it. These are:

- expectations

- resources

- accountability

- power.

Expectations

Most professional jobs carry high expectations of their work staff. With the advent of new technology, expectations on professionals have risen. Concern over the wear and tear of working long hours lay behind early social reforms including the eight-hour day and forty-hour week. Laws were established to ensure time for physical and mental recovery from work. Prior to the advent of advanced technology, we would work hard and put in long hours but would then go home and have some downtime to relax after work. Once out of the building we were able to switch off, unless we were on call.

Today it is very different. Many of us have a BlackBerry, iPhone or iPad, and consequently are expected to be available twenty-four hours a day for no extra pay. It is not unusual for employees to receive emails and phone calls well outside of office hours, and to be expected to respond to them. This is particularly true if we work in multinational companies and do global business. We feel the need to check for emails constantly, and are not really able to switch off mentally and forget about work.

The long hours worked by those in the stock market or by clergy who "live over" their work are now replicated by many other professionals, especially when they are away from their offices. Certain companies have a culture of being constantly available; to switch off your phone is viewed as being uncommitted and may hinder promotion. How are we to rest adequately when we have a constant influx of data? We check our gadgets at weekends, take them on holiday with us, and fear we will miss out if we do not look for messages daily. Such increased working hours and lack of regular time away from work are detrimental to our physical and emotional health.

A friend of ours went on holiday to Exmoor with his family, and was delighted to be unable to get a mobile signal because it meant that he could switch off from work when on holiday. Unsurprisingly, there are a number of studies that emphasize the importance of mentally distancing ourselves from work during non-work time in order to restore internal resources, depleted through work demands. To be able to switch off mentally is vitally important and is a protective factor against stress-related illness.[2] In fact, one of the symptoms of impending burnout is an inability to switch off from work and relax and unwind even when the opportunity is available. Among our interviewees, Heather's children told her she was obsessed with work to the point that she talked about it to the exclusion of all else. Justin couldn't distance himself from work even in school holidays. He found himself waking in the night, anxious about school issues.

Those who work in the caring professions face high expectations from three directions – from themselves, from their employers, and from the general public. And then there is a fourth direction – the home. Increased expectations in all these areas make it more difficult to achieve balanced lives.

Resources

Almost all organizations, whether they are in the private or public sector, are struggling with lack of money and therefore a lack of resources, while the same high level of service is expected. There is also often poor or inadequate support for workers: lack of administrative support, inadequate managerial support, possibly decreased training opportunities, and colleagues who cannot support each other because they are all fighting their own corner. Yet studies have shown that recovery from burnout is linked to increased job resources. A lack of adequate resources can lead to less job satisfaction and a sense of disengagement from the job.

For two of our interviewees, Suha and John, the administrative, clerical and secretarial support at work was lost owing to retirements and cost-cutting measures. This meant that they had to do many extra things – such as make phone calls and write letters – themselves, and this put more pressure on their time.

Accountability

Another factor that has changed in the workplace is accountability and bureaucracy. As one civil engineer said, "In the past, managers and administrators were there to help you with your work. Today they just measure what you do and tell you what you haven't done." While some of the changes have been good and for sound reasons, they have often led to hard-pressed teachers, social workers, police officers, health workers etc. spending disproportionate time completing paperwork that is largely unrelated to the job they trained to do. How this is managed in different settings depends on the leadership style of the service manager. If the manager has an upbeat, positive style, they are far more likely to take their workforce with them. If their style is to give negative feedback, this leads to further disillusionment and disengagement.

Austin started a new job and developed new projects. He became overwhelmed by the volume of work he had to do and worked longer and longer hours. Despite raising his concerns with his bosses, nothing was done to support him, and when some team members took annual leave, the added pressure tipped him over the edge. Richard adds, "Unlike my former secular employers, I did not find the church hierarchy supportive or helpful."

Power
Conflicts between the values of the organization and our personal ideals can also contribute to burnout, as was the case for John. He felt he compromised his own ideals, having to represent management policies he was not personally happy with.

Usually we go into a profession with high ideals and when our aims are thwarted by management and organizational dictats we are left with a degree of unpleasant dissonance between what we want to do and have always aspired to do in our job, and what is actually possible within the working environment. In her book *The Joy of Burnout* Dina Glouberman cites Professor Lloyd, who wrote, "Burnout occurs when your life has lost meaning within the structures you have committed to."[3] Loss of meaning and disengagement are big factors contributing to burnout.

Many in the workplace today feel they lack autonomy or the power to transform things. Often changes are imposed with no opportunity to contribute to the decision-making. This leads to people feeling demoralized and unimportant, with lack of certainty over their future and their inability to determine it. Idealism is compromised and people feel disempowered. John lost any sense of control when he had a new manager with very different goals who ignored his suggestions. The ethos of Ross's firm changed over time and the approach became much more callous and ruthless towards employees. Both John and Ross felt disempowered and unable to change their work practice.

Glenn Roberts writes: "Burnout is pre-eminently a disorder of the overcommitted and thwarted."[5]

LEGAL OBLIGATIONS OF EMPLOYERS

In the UK, employers are legally obliged to try to identify problems within their organization that might produce work-related stress. While they can expect their employees to withstand normal pressures of work, they have a duty to identify the sources of stress that could foreseeably cause an employee ill health and, if necessary, they should undertake preventative and protective action. The Health and Safety Executive can issue improvement notices to employers who fail to risk assess employees' exposure to work-related stress. This happened to a Health Trust, which after meeting the terms of the improvement notice was able to share its experiences with other Trusts.

In 2008, O2 Telecoms paid substantial damages to an accountant who suffered ill health due to working excessive hours and having a demanding workload. Although the accountant had mentioned her difficulties over a period of time and raised issues in appraisals, the managers did nothing significant to support her. They did not refer the employee to occupational health, nor provide any help to reduce the pressure. Inevitably the employee became ill with exhaustion.[4]

It is not surprising that this powerful cocktail of not caring for oneself adequately and feeling disillusioned and disengaged can produce burnout when combined with demands from family and friends and no space for downtime, recovery and recreation.

PART TWO

· · · · · · · · · · · · · · · · · ·

This second part of the book assumes you are burnt out or close to burnout. It offers some immediate help. The three chapters are based on a traffic lights motif. The first chapter is like "red" for stop. It is about how we can stop the harmful patterns of life which have burnt us out. The second is like "amber" for wait – having gained a bit of breathing space by stopping harmful things, how we can use that space to help us begin to recover. The third chapter is like "green" for go. It is about us starting to piece together a workable future to ensure we will not burn out again.

6

Red — I Am Burnt Out; How Can I Stop?

Interview: Nicola

Nicola was fifty-nine when she experienced burnout. She lives in France, working as a freelance translator and interpreter. She often travels overseas to translate at major conferences. She says:

I experienced a minor episode in the January of 2011, when I was acting as interpreter at a major conference, but also accepted a huge translation job at the same time. I suddenly found I couldn't sleep at all. I felt totally exhausted, emotionally fragile and tearful. After a period of total rest and some antidepressant medication I recovered enough to return to work.

That August, I had two sets of house guests at the same time, and began to worry about the mixture of people who were not comfortable together. My sleep became disrupted again. Then I took on a translation job [while] on holiday, which ran on into a retreat I was helping lead. This was particularly stressful as I had to keep going into the nearest village to get an Internet connection. Once I got back home, I was plunged into looking after two small grandchildren for a few days, coping with another house guest and preparing to head off for another important meeting. [Again] I became ... exhausted, stopped sleeping and was very tearful. I felt incredibly fragile. I was inert, lying around doing nothing. This time, despite huge support from my husband, a period in hospital, total rest and medication, recovery took a lot longer – many months.

I am now much more wary about taking on jobs and can say no more easily than before. I am learning to stop worrying about money, and recognize that I must not overdo it.

....

We are assuming that, having read the first part of the book, you believe you are burnt out to some degree. Maybe you are experiencing brownout, so still functioning but lacking zest for work, and probably everything else. You may have lost your idealism and energy and are just keeping going for the sake of it. Or you might be suffering from a more severe form of burnout, and are no longer able to function normally. You may have gone on long-term sick leave or lost your job through resigning or being sacked. If not in employment, then you may have lost other significant roles that you were fulfilling. Perhaps you are an exhausted mother who can no longer look after her children or a carer who can no longer care for a sick parent or other relative. You may have even needed hospitalization or medication to address your condition, as did Nicola, or contracted a medically recognized condition, as did Beth.

....

Interview: Beth

Beth is a family therapist working in the NHS. She burnt out when she was forty. She says:

I was working full-time and had a heavy and demanding caseload. My son had just started school at the age of five, and had finally been diagnosed with Autistic Spectrum Disorder and Attention Deficit Hyperactivity Disorder. He was active until late at night, had many anxieties and rigid routines, and needed a great deal of care and attention. One day I developed a sore throat, was given penicillin and within a few hours developed a very severe rash all over my body. I felt exhausted and I was tearful and weepy. Despite stopping the penicillin the rash didn't clear up, and I had to take time off work and have a course of steroids before I got better.

WHAT ARE WE GOING TO STOP?

There are four areas to consider when stopping the harmful things which have caused burnout or are causing brownout, and they operate at different levels.

Uppermost will be the need to stop overdoing it, to ease back on trying to do so much, to cut down on overwork.

Secondly, any burnout will have resulted from overwork that was driven by underlying, inner attitudes, and these too will need to change. Here we want to offer guidance on how to stop being so driven, so that we no longer blank out all other voices but the inner ones that drive us.

Thirdly, for some the experience of realizing they are in burnout is so shocking they feel it is the end of everything. They may attempt suicide or have strong urges to do so. Or they may sink into a depressive state, despairing of life. We give advice about how to stop feeling this way in this chapter. Instead of life having come to an end because of burnout, we argue that it could really be beginning. In this sense, burnout may turn out to be the best thing that has ever happened to us.

Finally, the immediate shock of realizing we are in burnout is usually accompanied by an overwhelming sense of personal failure. The same inner voices which have driven us to burnout are now telling us that not managing to fulfil their impossible demands makes us utter failures. We need to stop listening to such lies and start opening up to seeing issues of success and failure differently. So, to sum up, in this chapter we are going to suggest that we:

- Stop doing so much – indeed, stop being afraid of doing nothing.

- Stop running away from the truth of the situation – stop ignoring the warnings coming in from all around, and start heeding them.

- Stop thinking this is the end – have hope for a truer us to come out of this.

- Stop feeling a failure and regard burnout as an opportunity to regain a better life.

1. STOP DOING SO MUCH

We imagine that your life has been overfull for too long with work, maybe a sixty- to eighty-hour week, plus weekends. Here are three recent examples from the commuter village where we live.

A young father of three was taking one of his infant children to the toilet while on a family visit to the local swimming baths one Saturday morning. As he was bending over the lavatory, his BlackBerry slipped out of his pocket into the toilet pan and proved unworkable after it was rescued. "The best weekend I've had in ages," he said.

I (Andrew) couldn't sleep and got up at four-thirty in the morning to send out some emails. I got a shock to receive a reply from one of our City trader friends. He was already at his desk.

I later went to talk to a young mother in a professional family and suggested I meet her and her husband one week night. She gave a snort of derision and said, "He's too tired to talk to me, let alone you, of an evening once he finally gets in! We only talk at weekends."

Such overwork is common – we know. As we said earlier, we have become burnt out too. So you need to stop, to allow yourself some space to do nothing much.

Stopping with burnout

You may have had little choice about stopping work, and therefore had an abrupt change of lifestyle from a life overfull with pressured work to nothing. No commute, no office, no one depending on you, nothing to fill the empty days.

Ironically, you may well miss some of the upside of your working life, even though until you had to stop you had come to hate it. You can miss the sense of involvement, the activity, the adrenalin rush; having your days mapped out and not having too much time to think. Ross says that "although work burned me out, the paradox is that some elements built me up". He recognized how much his self-esteem had been tied into his being successful in the workplace.

If you are a man used to being out to work, you may feel guilty being around the house. You want to prove yourself useful by helping out. Also, the best partner in the world won't be able to stop themselves from being worried for you and for the overall situation, especially if there are dependent children involved. They too will have to make abrupt adjustments to their lifestyle, which will show in both big and small ways.

When Ross found himself at home and under his wife's feet, the enforced rest was a blow to his ego and he wondered if he would ever work again. You may be tempted to show the world that you are not down and out and still have some get up and go, and want to keep busy. Some people almost recreate the pressure they were in at work by throwing themselves into a new big project, such as building an extension or redecorating the house. Others, worried by the loss of income, put their house on the market and begin making far-reaching plans for downsizing.

These may be right things to do in the longer term, but we suggest, at the very first, it is vital to cut yourself some slack and not be afraid to do nothing much. If spending time slumped in front of daytime TV, getting up late, sleeping on the sofa or going for a walk is all you can manage, you shouldn't be fazed. Body, mind and soul are beginning to relax after years of overstress. If it seems too much to think about anything, that is fine.

We were once so tired on a holiday in France that we slept for about ten hours each night. Andrew had had to cope with two awful scandals, one in his church and one in the school where he was chair of governors (not involving him personally), and Elizabeth had had a tough time in her NHS work. Then when we had got up, swum in the pool, and bought and eaten our croissants, we went back to bed and slept until lunchtime, two more hours. We did that for ten of the fourteen days, until we had recovered enough not to need the further morning sleep. It felt odd but it was very much the right thing to do.

Don't worry if recovery seems to take a long time. Burnout may have built up over a good number of years, possibly your entire working career. You need space to do nothing at all taxing and to take it easy.

You need to be unafraid of doing nothing and chilling out. You might do jigsaws, watch TV, sleep a lot or take the dog for long walks. These things are achieving a great deal: doing nothing, you are allowing time to heal you. The time will come for rebuilding and re-establishing a routine. For now, just allow your body, mind and spirit to start to recuperate.

Stopping with brownout

Everything we have said so far applies to those who have had to leave their work or role of responsibility. What about those with brownout who have not stopped or cannot stop altogether? We advise cutting down as much as possible, and suggest you:

- don't give up on the job but take your lunch hour
- take all the annual leave due to you
- leave work on time
- refuse to be contactable during time off unless formally on call
- take proper sick leave if ill.

Find things that are not work-related to alleviate the working day:

- read a novel on the commute
- read it some more in your lunch break
- take some fresh air at some stage
- go to the gym
- listen to music
- meet a friend.

As we have seen earlier, Justin found his own solutions after researching stress management. He

- planned positive activities such as holidays to look forward to
- worked hard at keeping issues in perspective
- listened to music or read light books when he was unable to sleep
- became more sanguine about lack of sleep.

Justin is sure that without strategies like these he would have burnt out. His symptoms gradually reduced as he got the measure of the job.

If brownout is caused by bad relationships at work, seek to minimize conflict and learn to lie low, to let stuff go past. Try not to respond. It's not worth it. You want to be bothered about those who love you, not some work colleague you had never met before taking this job and want never to meet again once you leave it. Maybe it's not as simple as that. We deal with conflict in relationships in Chapter 9 but, very broadly, we advise letting as much as possible pass by. It's only work.

We can hear the hollow laughter at many of these suggestions. We know that many will seem quite remote. You may say that taking all the time off that you are due, including annual leave, weekends and lunch breaks would mark you out, maybe even endanger your job. Or it would mean you could not do the job properly. If so, start small. Find five minutes in the working day to be yourself.

Case History: Paul

Paul was a teacher who came to see Andrew because of brownout verging on burnout. He feared a total breakdown and felt suicidal at times. He couldn't leave his job, because his family needed the income. Andrew made the suggestions written above only for Paul to dismiss them as impossible. Then he suggested Paul take just five minutes in his car in the school car park before going into the buildings. He screwed up his face for a moment and said that should just be possible. He was a man of his word and did take that five minutes – he used it for meditative prayer. It proved the turning point for him. After further regular meetings, his attitude became less negative. It was not long before he was able to retire happily, do some supply teaching, and fill the rest of his life with long abandoned creative pursuits.

Great oaks from little acorns grow. It could be that, like Paul, taking a little time could start a full release. Consider what the alternative is if you do not start to do something differently, and who it will impact apart from you. If you are currently facing brownout and you don't make changes, however small, the chances are that sooner or later you will face burnout, and then you will have to stop completely. You will simply not be able to go on any longer. Offering yourself up as a sacrifice to a career you are no longer enjoying is crazy. You have to start to change somewhere, however small at first.

2. STOP RUNNING AWAY FROM THE TRUTH OF THE SITUATION

In addition to overactivity, burnout has an element of denial. Indeed, you may well have been in denial in a big way to get burnt out or browned out.

We have all met the person who can't admit the reality of something unpleasant to them and so deny it. It can be about something superficial, such as the unbeatable nature of their favourite football team, or that Italian food is the only way to eat out properly. In these instances, denial might be no more than an endearing foible, but when denial is used about serious issues in life, it can be extremely damaging.

If you are burnt out, warning messages and signals were coming in from all sides but you were not listening to them.

- **Your body** – you felt under the weather, were susceptible to lots of minor illnesses such as colds, and suffered from headaches. You may not have understood what your body was saying to you. When you still would not listen, you became more unwell. You may have suffered from some serious conditions, like Beth's severe rash, or Margaret's chronic fatigue – all diseases linked to overstress.

- **Your unconscious mind** – you couldn't sleep properly and were having disturbing dreams.

- **Your conscious mind** – you had concentration lapses and became restless and hazy.

- **Your family and friends** – they either told you directly or dropped hints, and you ignored all of them.

This is denial.

Some people deny that anything bad is happening, and pretend everything is OK. Others suppress the truth and avoid thinking about it, making excuses or promising themselves that as soon as this project is over or that deadline is met, they will reassess what is happening. And they can also promise those around them that they are going to change things, but they never actually do. If you are burnt out, you have acknowledged all the danger signals you were receiving, but suppressed them because you wanted to achieve your goal.

It is important here to recall Ed's message to those suffering with burnout. He said individuals have to recognize for themselves what is happening, and that all too often we don't recognize it until it is too late. It's important to ask yourself if you have a supportive network around you and whether you have empowered them to give you honest feedback. If you have, are you receptive to it?

To continue the process of recovery:

- stop ignoring the warnings

- listen to your body

- listen to your mind – both conscious and unconscious

- listen to your family and friends

- take their advice.

We give a lot of helpful techniques to start the process of getting out of the cycle of denial and suppression as the book goes on, but for now, be content just to make the bare intention to stop these ways of thinking.

3. STOP THINKING THIS IS THE END

Suicidal thoughts

Burnout affects our thinking and feeling. Our thinking may become distorted, very negative and pessimistic: "I'm hopeless and I've let everyone down. I'm a failure. I am a burden to my family. I hate myself, so everyone else must hate me too. I may as well be dead; no one will miss me."

This can be how you feel and think, even though it isn't the truth. If you are having such dark thoughts, ending it all can seem a very attractive way out. You think you are being logical, but your thinking is irrational. There have been several successful suicides by people working in the financial world, who were under great stress. Suicide can be a real danger.

As I (Andrew) was preparing this section of our book, I was given a suicide note written by a forty-eight-year-old man. It ran to several pages. It was lucid. It was caring in tone. He had been a successful businessman. Things had gone wrong. There had been a takeover at the company and the politics had changed. He was unjustly dismissed. The one phrase out of the entire letter to strike me the hardest was: "I cannot live with failure."

I became suicidal some years ago when the politics of my church became toxic. I took to sitting staring at the wall of the guest bedroom half the night. Suicide began to seem the most natural thing in the world, the obvious solution. Mercifully, I had enough detachment left to talk to Elizabeth. I got professional help. The danger was avoided. After a six-week break from work I was able to return and the danger of suicide never recurred. The thought that I might have put my family through such permanent suffering, scarring them for life, and lost my own life for the sake of some church issues now seems unthinkable, but at the time it did not.

We implore anyone who is having suicidal thoughts because of burnout to take them seriously and get help. Talk to someone you trust: a close family member or friend, a counsellor or a GP. It doesn't matter who as long as you tell someone. You could contact the Samaritans, who are excellent. Their contact details are in the Resources section. Usually, it is a relief to share such worrying thoughts, and the person you confide in can help or, if not, can at least pass you on to someone who can. Recovering from burnout reduces suicidal thoughts, and you need to hold on to that.

4. STOP FEELING A FAILURE

Having to stop work because your health has broken down can lead to you feeling your whole life has been a failure. This can be very crushing on top of all the other failures that led to the burnout. It is possible that fear of failure was instrumental in allowing the burnout to creep up on you in the first place. If that is so, it is time to take stock and realize that you are not a failure. No one comes to the point of burnout without having put in years and years of very sacrificial, highly skilled work in difficult circumstances, under which no one could succeed. Gifted, idealistic, self-sacrificial people are most susceptible to burnout. Before ultimately and inevitably burning out, they will have probably done marvellous things.

In fact, deciding to stop living in such a driven, blinkered and destructive way cannot be a failure. It is a success to stop living like that. Failure would have been to carry on, and those who do manage to keep on living like that often become almost subhuman as people – insensitive and ruthless, quite dehumanized. The success is to stop, to realize that you are a human being, fallible and with limits. Life is not all about achieving, under the terms that you may have believed when you were so driven. Don't think of yourself as a failure, but as a highly gifted human being who has achieved great things but has finally come to a point where your outlook needs to change. That is why you are reading these words now. You are on the brink of exciting new possibilities. Now is your chance to change, to make new choices.

Like you, we have been there, and we know that we can all learn from our mistakes. We can celebrate what we did that was right and also that which was wrong but done with good motives. We can keep what is good. We can get rid of what was bad. We can start again. We can redefine our lives. We can put our old values to the test and adapt them, weed them out, jettison what we wish, bring in new things. Most likely there will be a less wholesale set of changes than might at first be imagined. We are still ourselves. It is likely that gentle, gradual change will soon encourage us to start our life over again.

In fact, you would do well to view stopping the patterns of burnout as perhaps the biggest opportunity of your life so far. It means you can

- do things differently, and get off that treadmill that was tiring you to the point of exhaustion

- look at all the many other things that life offers

- deepen your relationships, and love and receive love from those around you more sensitively

- explore major matters of culture, spirituality, creativity and thought

- use your great giftings in a more measured way that will make you more grateful when it comes to the end of your life and you look back.

This is the value of stopping. It is the first step on the way to recovery. In fact, burnout is not at all the end but, properly addressed, it is the beginning of a new way of looking at life which is far healthier, less driven, and altogether saner. We need to see life not in all-or-nothing terms but as a place where we will make mistakes – big ones – but can forgive ourselves and carry on.

7

Amber — I Am Burnt Out;
....
What Can I Do?
....

CREATING SPACE FOR OURSELVES

You have already heard part of Ross's story in Chapter 4, where we described how he burnt out and had to stop working. Here is the remainder of his story about how it was after he had stopped work.

Interview: Ross, part two

I was surprised to find how supportive friends and even former clients were. I felt I would be a pariah, but people's support was a major part of my rehabilitation. I slept a lot, didn't take anything on and began to talk about my problems with my wife, my local vicar and a psychiatrist. Then, fifteen months later, I got a new job with a smaller company that had a different work ethos and put less pressure on their workforce.

I recognized how much my self-esteem had been tied into my being successful in the workplace. Overall I feel to have gained from the experience. I had time to really get to know my two small children. I am determined to keep time boundaries and not measure my effectiveness in hours worked. I can see that although my working day is two hours shorter, I am working better. I have become more honest with myself and with other people, and have learned not to bottle things up but to talk about them.

CHANGING LIGHT

The light has changed to amber. You are not ready to get going again but you have time to prepare for it. You have a little space for waiting.

We often speak of "breathing space" or of "having a breather", and part of this chapter will concentrate on our breathing. Under prolonged overstress, we can often get into the habit of breathing too shallowly and swallowing too much air. We shall be looking at ways to relax our breathing, slow down and create some space in order to feel less hemmed in by life. In his article "Burnout – a personal journey" B. Gaede writes that "the process of recovering from burnout is a slow journey that needs time and space".[1]

The sections that follow are only guidelines. Life is one organic whole and the sections interconnect, so feel free to mix them up – take stuff from one bit and use it with bits from another. It's what works best that matters. We are going to offer three sections. They are:

- **Giving ourselves emotional space.** We need to reverse our habitual, emotional harshness and start being kind to ourselves. Then we need to find a pleasant and healthy recuperative routine. Finally, we suggest an emotional exercise called the "safe place" exercise. It is widely used in therapy and designed to help us have an inner well of good, up-building, emotional resources to draw on when we feel bad.

- **Giving ourselves physical space.** We need to look at our bodies. We may have chronic physical tension, and we shall look at various things that could help us relax physically. Then we need to improve our physical environment, making it more restorative. It will have been neglected along with everything else while we were busy burning out.

- **Giving ourselves mental space.** Our minds will have been in chronic overdrive, full of data, deadlines and pressure. We shall look at ways to calm our minds, to allow ourselves to think straight and to create inner space. This should help us feel less chaotic, more orderly, more at peace with ourselves. There are four ways to achieve this – simple meditation, reflection, pausing and writing. They are all time-honoured, proven ways to still the mind, and they can be blended in whatever mix you find the most helpful.

I. GIVING OURSELVES EMOTIONAL SPACE

Being kind to ourselves

It sounds simple and obvious, doesn't it? Why be anything else but kind to ourselves? But in fact many, many people, especially those suffering burnout, drive themselves on remorselessly. We beat ourselves up mentally. We have lacerating inner messages about how lazy, stupid and generally useless we are. We make ourselves overwork to levels of exhaustion and still feel we are not doing enough. We blame ourselves for everything that goes wrong. We cut out pleasures to try to compensate for things not going to plan, a plan which was dangerously ambitious anyway. And so on and so on. We are our own jailers and slave drivers.

Dina Glouberman says, "Few burnout people have any regard for their own needs and wishes... Our willingness to ignore our own welfare can lead us to situations which are actually abusive."[2]

In the last chapter we decided to stop all that. We are now in a waiting place between stopping and getting going again, and we are going to start learning to be kind to ourselves.

Treats

Think of ways to treat yourself regularly – maybe daily, or every other day; certainly once a week. Treats needn't involve lots of money or time, but are something that you really enjoy. Or better, several somethings. Make a list of easy things that you would really enjoy and have not allowed yourself to do, with all the pressure of life:

- have a long, hot, luxurious bath

- enjoy a cup of your favourite coffee

- read or reread a novel

- have a massage

- go for a swim or jog or walk

- eat a favourite snack

- watch a favourite TV programme or film

- go to the cinema or theatre.

The important thing is to punctuate your life now with feel-good things; allow yourself to feel human again, and to know that you deserve to be treated well.

These are small things. You may consider something bigger like a good, long holiday or even a sabbatical period, but these take money and time and so may not be possible. It might be best to delay taking them in any case until your energy levels have recovered sufficiently to make the most of them. For now, we suggest getting into the habit of putting regular, simple, affordable and pleasant things into your life.

Creating a healthy routine

After a time of stopping, and on the assumption that you are beginning to feel better than at the red light for stop stage, there will begin to come a need for a routine. This will be particularly important if your life has been so radically changed because of burnout that the old life has completely gone. We all need a routine; indeed, we tend to create it for ourselves even when we need not do so. For instance, on holiday when we have no firm plans, we still end up creating a routine for the day – even if it is a very lazy one. We shop at the same time, swim at the same time, go to the beach at the same time each day and so on.

Now we will think about establishing a routine that works for you. All the guidelines we have been giving so far, and will continue to give, about looking after yourself, not pushing it and being gentle, still apply as you set up your routine.

Emerging routine

Hopefully one will emerge rather than need to be constructed from scratch. We are wonderful creatures and if we give ourselves half a chance we can find much healing from within. Our bodies, minds and emotions will find their own healthy tempo if they are allowed to within a sensible overall life-view. You will begin to decide things to do routinely each day. It may start with one thing – that morning constitutional around the park starts showing its worth, so you build it in as a daily thing by instinct. After the walk, you sit down and relax for a while. This creates routine.

Doing a little work

At some stage, you will want to do some jobs again. This does not mean going back to your previous job under the same circumstances, but something else, hopefully something more creative for you, perhaps drawn from the array of creative ideas we give later. Probably you are not able to have the whole of your time free. There are jobs which need doing to keep the household going. If you live in a conventional nuclear family, there will be school runs, shopping, looking after the children, cleaning, ironing and the like. It would be good to build a decent modicum of such work into your daily routine. The curse of such chores leading up to burnout is that they have to be fitted in on top of a very pressured job. If you are off work then they can give pleasure, or at least help you feel justified in taking your pleasures.

Committing it to paper

It may help if you write your routine down. People differ about having written routines. Some find them liberating, others find them restrictive. It may be good to have a wall planner, or it may not. Each person will need to find their own way of doing things. The same applies to how detailed the routine is. Some people enjoy most of their time being accounted for; others want a lot of gaps when they don't know what will happen, so they can remain flexible.

Personality preferences

Still another variable will be your personal preferences. We look into these more fully in Chapter 10, but, for example, some people are extroverts who derive energy from being with other people. Others are introverts who get energy from solitude.

At the early stage of burnout, we are too tired to do anything but flop, as we do when we are ill. But as energy returns, even a little, you might need to be aware of which type of person you are. It's no good an extrovert planning a routine of solitary things, no matter how nice they seem in themselves. An extrovert needs to get out and meet others in some way, or they will wilt. The introvert will need to build in loads of solitude when in recovery from burnout. So you will need to be aware of this preference among several others.

Your routine will need to be checked out with any others in your family or those with whom you share your life, to make sure it fits with their needs too.

Creating a "safe place"

This exercise is one of the most useful ones in therapy. We strongly recommend it. It builds a place of emotional retreat to which we can have recourse at any time when we are under stress.

Stephen's experience

Stephen is a self-employed builder with plenty of business and financial worries, living alone. He is estranged from his partner, who has taken their son, a six-year old, to another country where communications are poor. His only way to talk to his son is by mobile phone at great expense, at a certain time of the week, which his ex-partner changes at whim. She also tells him, when he does ring, the boy doesn't want to talk to him, even after Stephen has built his whole day around holding the conversation. He finds the time after a conversation with his son, however it has gone, very upsetting, and as a result he can rarely do much for the rest of the day. He has found using the "safe place" a good recourse after putting the phone down. He is now able to recover and get on with his day, after a few minutes, even if he remains in some emotional pain.

We recommend using the "safe place" technique for easing the perpetual emotional strain of burnout or brownout. It can be used equally well for a general easing of the overall tension or for particularly hurtful aspects of any recurring circumstances.

The "safe place" technique

Imagine yourself in a place that you would define as most safe and secure, the furthest away from the problems that have led to burnout or any other problems you might have. It can be real or it can be imagined. You can be on your own or with others. It could be on a beach in Honolulu, mountaineering in the Himalayas, in a canoe on the Amazon, having a coffee in Starbucks – almost anything. But imagine yourself there, and take your time over it. Work your way round your five senses.

What can you see? What can you hear? What can you smell? What can you touch? What can you taste? Allow this to build up in your mind until it takes a grip on your emotions, and you are there in your imagination. Stay there as long as you like or have time for. When you are ready, come back to reality as gently as you can. This is a sort of emotional meal that nourishes our emotions when we are starving for the good things. It sets us up to face our issues.

2. GIVING OURSELVES PHYSICAL SPACE

Relaxing from chronic bodily tension
The process that leads to burnout tends to make us lose the ability to relax, and our minds and bodies race on. Stopping feels artificial and uncomfortable. Do not be surprised or dismayed at this. When we do stop after being unnaturally overstimulated for a long time, then we realize how wound up we are.

Any physical exercise is good for relaxing and balancing your outlook on life, as long as you don't overdo it too early in your recovery. We recommend making exercise part of your routine. Clearly the type and amount of exercise will differ a great deal from person to person and needs some thought.

We recommend the use of one or more of any number of the excellent relaxation techniques and aids that are available. We give two of the best we have come by in the Resources section. There are many others in any book shop, library, music shop and online.

Here is a simple relaxation technique:

Lie flat on the floor or sit in a chair in an alert but relaxed position. Beginning with your toes, concentrate on each muscle group in your body. Tense your toes; curl them up for a few seconds and then slowly and gently relax them. Then, with the rest of the foot, curl it tight and then relax. Next, become conscious of your shins and do the same, tensing the calf muscles and then relaxing, and so on all the way up your body. Do your knees and thighs and hips, your belly and hands, forearms, elbows, upper arms, chest, shoulders, neck, jaw, facial muscles and finally the scalp. This exercise should take ten to fifteen minutes, and should be practised three times a day. It can be combined with meditation or listening to music. It can be done outdoors in the right weather conditions. Some people prefer to do it either naked or wearing very little, which adds a sensuous side to it, but it can be done fully clothed equally well.

If you do this regularly, you will find that you become more relaxed.

Creating more pleasant physical surroundings

Pressure of work may have led you to neglect your immediate surroundings, your home and garden. Or you may have had to change home and circumstances because of burnout; it may have gone hand in hand with a divorce or separation, and you may have lost a lovely living space and have to manage with something less pleasant. But whatever your circumstances, we suggest putting some thought into improving the physical space in which you live. If you are too tired to redecorate, or cannot afford it, there are other things you can do: putting some flowers in a vase, sorting through a backlog of papers and going through long-neglected drawers and cupboards, maybe changing ornaments around and making the room look different in one way or another. It could be doing some spring cleaning, even if it is not spring. If you have a garden, especially if it has been neglected, you might like to tidy it up. If funds run to it, get some new plants and shrubs.

It is important not to let these things be a burden. The whole point of doing them is enjoyment and to create a nicer space for you to live in. If you are very tired we suggest only doing as much as you have energy for. You may need to do a little and then stop. Be patient and gentle with yourself. In time, the energy will begin to flow back. Avoid desperate work in house or garden just to find significance after losing your job. We are significant simply by being ourselves.

A special place

You can go further and create a special place where you are going to sit and be especially thoughtful and meditative, because the place in which we relax in a focused way is important. You may be fortunate enough to have a room that you can dedicate to being such a place. Otherwise, it may need to be a part of a room where you make a focal point, such as a coffee table with a candle or a sculpture or a bowl of flowers or some other things of quiet beauty (shells, pebbles or driftwood are good). Perhaps a piece of artwork that you find meaningful could be the focus, or if you belong to a particular faith, one of its symbols could be displayed in a decorative way that is pleasing to you.

However it is prepared, it is going to be a special place where you can try to relax deeply in your mind and soul, and meditate. It helps in meditation if a consistent place can be used regularly, and if it is beautifully prepared, so a place of sanctuary will be created.

3. GIVING OURSELVES MENTAL SPACE

Meditation: Mindfulness

The evidence that meditation helps in times of stress of all kinds is overwhelming. Many of the world's religions have developed ways to meditate to bring the individual closer to their spiritual centre. In so doing, meditation has been found to reduce stress. It has been proven to help in the therapeutic world too.

Matthew Johnstone is a writer and cartoonist who has battled for over twenty years with depression. His short, funny cartoon book *I Had a Black Dog* became an international best-seller. He has recently written a new book, *Quiet the Mind,* to explain how meditation has helped him. He says, "I don't know the meaning of life, but I do know that life is so much better when I meditate."[3]

We strongly recommend trying some simple meditation as a way out of burnout. Meditation is a vast field. There are all kinds of different ways to do it. We give a couple of good starting points in the Resources section but here is a basic meditation technique called Mindfulness, which is about consciously paying attention to the present moment in an accepting way. It is a capacity that we already possess and it doesn't require specific religious or cultural beliefs. There is a lot of research to show Mindfulness decreases stress levels and increases a sense of well-being.[4]

How to meditate and practise Mindfulness

How does Mindfulness work? In very simple terms, it proposes that we have two states of mind that respond to things happening in our environment – a conceptual one which labels, analyses, judges, plans, remembers and reflects, and one which is more direct and needs all of our senses to experience what is going on. Mindfulness seeks to direct our attention to the experiential state of mind, and to train our attention to become more aware of the present moment. We are asked to simply focus on noticing what is there and accepting it. Although it sounds and is simple, it is not easy, but it does produce very positive results in well-being for those who practise it.

Try this simple exercise. Adopt the same position as for relaxation, either flat out on your back or seated in a chair in an alert posture. Have both feet on the floor, hands resting on the knees, palms up, feet slightly apart, bottom pushed to the back of the chair, back upright, head upright, alert but relaxed. Then concentrate on noticing your breathing, trying to switch the mind off to all else. Don't exaggerate your breathing; there is no need to breathe particularly deeply or shallowly, just keep the breathing at the normal rate but focus on it. You don't need to think about it but simply notice it, and enter into its steady silent rhythm, resting the brain in all other regards. Simply notice breathing in and out, in and out, in and out and nothing else. Start by doing this for a couple of minutes and gradually build up to twenty minutes, three times a day.

Another way

Another option is to focus on what you can hear. This means you will notice sounds that would have been missed without a specific focus. They might be lovely sounds like birdsong or the cry of children outside, or they might be quite abrasive – the sound of traffic or building site noises. It doesn't matter. Focus on the sounds to the exclusion of all else, almost travelling in your mind's eye to the source of the sound, allowing yourself to become absorbed in it, and then travelling back again.

Both these techniques use your senses, and you may want to think about all that you can see, hear, touch, smell, taste and feel where your body is right now. This is a beginning of Mindfulness.

Wandering minds

When we try to meditate like this, all kinds of other thoughts crowd in. Our mental life seems like pandemonium. We try to still our brain but it just freewheels all over the place. We find ourselves thinking about the shopping, wanting to get on with the jobs we have lined up for ourselves, going back over what we saw on TV last night, and a thousand and one other things. Our attention has been likened to an untrained puppy. Puppies wander around sniffing aimlessly; they don't stay where they should, they make messes and they bring back things you didn't ask for. They need training, and we need to train our wandering minds. When we recognize our mind is wandering, we need gently to bring it back to our focus – if necessary, over and over again.

You are not likely to feel calm, meditative and centred immediately, but no matter, persist. We suggest disciplining yourself to stay there for at least five minutes, however uncomfortable and unrewarding it seems, but no longer than twenty minutes as a beginner. Try to meditate/be mindful at least once a day. This would very much depend on your circumstances and aptitude. Don't look for results straight away. Do the meditation, whether it feels good or bad, and then do something else.

Most people who practise meditation begin to notice a benefit after about a week or so – not in the meditation session, but at other times. They may realize they are behaving more calmly, have more time to react in situations, and life seems less hassled. This is good; the evidence that meditation is beneficial in helping us to relax and avoid overstressing ourselves is incontrovertible. Meditation techniques using the breath suggest that we think of breathing in good things, and breathing out our stress, our tension, our failures, our sense of disappointment and our regrets. There is no need to make a particular construction like this on your breathing though, unless you find it helpful.

As we mentioned above, many meditation techniques are linked to religious belief. They focus on receiving the help and goodness and guidance of whoever we have faith in, with each breath.

The habit of reflection

The next technique we recommend in creating good mental space is reflection. This is similar to both relaxing and meditating, but is distinct and can be combined with them. The basic exercise involved is to run your mind back over the last twenty-four hours. Do this in a very relaxed and free way, not as an intense memory exercise. It is a free-floating, almost casual run back through the previous day. It is often done last thing at night in bed or as a way of going to sleep.

Think of the best thing that has happened in the last twenty-four hours. What struck you for good? Often the answer is a surprise:

not something you had planned or worked for, but something unexpected, such as a cashier at a supermarket being pleasant when she might have been short, or a snatch of birdsong, a child running into school from their parent's car and looking so happy with the world. It can be almost anything, but it has touched you in some way. Dwell on it and allow all the goodness to soak into you. Remember it, holding the memory in your mind's eye, until it has no more savour and can do you no more good.

Do not rush this. It is surprising how long thinking something through like that can take. You should savour it like a sweet on the tongue, easing it around your memory as you would ease the sweet round your mouth, allowing its full flavour time to permeate the memory. You need to resist the temptation to crunch up the memory and swallow it too soon, just like you shouldn't crunch up the sweet and swallow it. You need to allow it to melt away of its own accord.

By the time you have done that with your first memory, there will probably be other good things which now come to your notice. You can then go on to reflect on them in the same way.

Even if life is really a torture at the moment and each day seems like agony, it's a rare day with nothing good in it at all. Often we let the good slip by us when we are experiencing hardship and tension. We become inured to the bad and maximize that instead of the good. Reflecting reverses that and allows us to draw the most benefit from all the good that there has been in the day. It's quite possible that you have got to the end of the day and thought "Another dreary bad day in a life of dreary bad days" but on reflection, there have been some lovely things. Maybe they were not *that* lovely, and there were not that many of them, but they were there and they are important to dwell on. If you are in an emotional desert, it's important to gather up all the nourishment and refreshment you can, just as if you were in a real desert, where you would maximize every drop of water for as long as you could and savour it on your tongue.

The practice of pausing

This exercise is designed to combat the state of permanent rush we feel if we have suffered burnout. Society as a whole expects rapid responses, with its instant information technology and much else. We feel under pressure to do things immediately. This is OK up to a point, but we will have long ago passed that point if we are in burnout. It's time to stop and "stand and stare" as the well-known poem has it.

I (Andrew) was once fortunate enough to have a month's sabbatical, which I spent walking the Yorkshire Dales. It was a lovely and spiritually profound time. One rule I had was that I would stop and sit down for five minutes on any bench I passed as I was walking. It proved a good rule but very hard to do. Even when I had no real time deadlines, when the whole day was my own, I still resisted stopping and having five minutes' pause on the relatively infrequent country benches. I wanted to get on. I had a plan. I had mapped a progress chart of the day in my head and wanted to stick to it. But it was good to make myself pause, and, looking back, it was those times of sitting reflectively on the benches that furnished me with some of my most emotionally nourishing memories.

So we recommend building pauses into life. Start by noticing when something in your day has touched you in some way. It might be anything – a view, a kind word, an amusing thought, a happy memory. If you can, as it is happening, pause to drink it in properly. If you are walking the dog early one winter's morning and notice the sunrise, pause there, drinking in that lovely thing. Don't be tempted to rush on. Inner voices will be pulling you away from the spot, telling you that time is short. Ignore them and take time appreciating the wonder of the sunrise. Only move on when all its goodness has been exhausted. It will be surprising how short a time it takes, probably only a couple of minutes, but it will have felt longer. And it will have slowed your pace.

Dina Glouberman says, "Joy emerges in the spaces rather than in the content of our lives. It is what happens when, even for a moment, we feel totally free, with a sense of space around us and inside us."[5] This is the importance of pausing. It allows space for life's joys to touch us.

Another useful time to pause is when something unexpectedly good happens. Again, it may only be something small – the receptionist at the doctor's is pleasant and your appointment can be fitted in conveniently. When you leave the surgery, pause and let the fortunate circumstances have their effect. We tend to expect things to go wrong, especially so when we are depressed, overstressed, and burnt out. But life is not all bad. There are blessings all along the way if we will but look for them and then take the proper time to appreciate them.

If you genuinely cannot pause at the moment of receiving the good thing, then pause when next you can – before getting out of the car, or before starting the next email. Just pause long enough to let the good event sink into your mind and your feelings.

Even if you do not seem to have good things happening much, still we suggest making a practice of pausing. Take a moment between things. Pause before entering a building. Pause before getting into the car. Pause before eating a meal, maybe for a moment of thankfulness but also to slow down. Pause before leaving the table. Pause before making a phone call, especially if it's to a loved one, or to handle a tricky subject. Pause in any way, anywhere. Punctuate the day with little pauses and derive the benefit of easing down the pace of life, of noticing things more, and appreciating all the good life has to offer.

We realize that pausing blends with reflection and meditation. They are brothers and sisters to each other. We can interplay them at leisure. Together they build towards an altogether happier and healthier way to live life each day.

Writing: keeping a journal or blog

Finally we recommend writing things down as a key way to recover mental space from burnout.

Writing is very good for us. Its therapeutic value is well researched. It helps us get things sorted out in our minds, especially in times of suffering when life seems so out of control and chaotic. Writing is cathartic, an excellent way to channel pain, to externalize it. It is also reconciling: once we have written about something, especially if it is painful, the act of writing can help us be reconciled to what has happened. Writing is empowering: probably through the good effects just mentioned, it seems to have a facility for helping the writer feel they have potency and significance. This is especially healing when we feel a victim of distressing events which have put us down and made us feel failures or worthless in some way.

In addition to these good effects, writing is permanent. It can be returned to and reassessed. It can be reconsidered before it is passed on to another, though initially it is also absolutely private and need only be shared if we wish it to be. There is no need to censor what we want to say for fear of its effect on a hearer. All these factors give it the edge over speech.

Writing goes emotionally deeper than the spoken word. People usually find they surprise themselves with the things they write. It seems to have the power to reveal stronger reactions to our circumstances than we had realized just by thinking or speaking about them. It can evoke significant memories that we had suppressed because of their strength. Writing searches the soul and allows us to dialogue with our inner self in a unique way.

Ed attributes getting better to keeping a reflective diary, reading and understanding what was happening to him. A friend suggested he try writing down what he thought his purpose was in life. The writing process led him into an important reassessment of his values, which itself led to his recovery from burnout. Writing can be especially helpful as part of the journey to recovery.

Don't be put off writing

Many people were put off writing at school. They may have had a bad experience in English classes, feel they can't write, can't spell, don't know grammar, won't know what to say. None of this matters in the slightest. It's not school. It's you getting better. You are not going to be marked on it. You can't write the wrong thing. Whatever you write is going to be significant. If you end up copying out the telephone directory as your way of writing, then that is significant. But that is not likely. You will write truly important thoughts that will be really helpful to you.

Buy an attractive journal at the stationers, one that appeals to you, and get a good pen. Or if you are a keyboard person, use your PC, laptop or iPad, and start a blog. But however you choose to write, take care that it is safe from prying eyes and cannot be inadvertently discovered.

How and what to write

It is ideal to write for twenty minutes at a time, preferably daily, but if that is not possible, then at least twice a week. We are aware that with the relaxation and meditation this is beginning to sound like a lot of time and you may need to prioritize, particularly if you are still in work or have other major commitments. However, we find in our therapeutic work that people tend either to get going and find benefit from all these techniques or don't get going at all.

One way to start is to put into the written word what you have reflected on. You may not want to write about something good; it may be something that has caused pain and difficulty, and that is OK. You may not want to write factual things, so it is fine to write a story, a poem or a fantasy. It is good to make a written note of your journey to recovery too, by keeping a diary recording the basic shape of each day and your feelings about it. Looking back later can help you get a good idea of how your recovery is going. However, it need not be a daily diary. Occasional notes about important stages in the fight for recovery can be good. They cement the fact that you are getting better into your mind more strongly for being written down.

For Michael, whose full story finishes off our book, two things in particular helped him get better. One was using a journal to record and process his journey. He says, "My journal became like a friend to me during those weeks and months…In those early weeks when I couldn't speak very much I felt it was easier to write my questions, hurts and prayers."

As you take time to build vital breathing space, you can start to look towards actively working on your recovery.

8

Green — I Am Burnt Out; Where Did I Go Wrong?

LOOKING BACK AND LEARNING

Having accepted the situation you find yourself in, of burnout or brownout, and having created some emotional and physical space and begun to relax, the third step in overcoming it is to look back over what led to it and learn from any mistakes. This is the green light – time to set off again. It may be very slow going at first, but that doesn't matter. It is important to go at your own pace, tackling only what can be managed at any one time. What come next are simply guidelines: feel free to pick and choose.

THINKING BACK

Before you start, it is important to realize that your situation will not be a total disaster. Major things have gone wrong, but others have gone right. You will not have lost everything. Much that is good will remain. There is a danger that we can see things too much in black and white, viewing ourselves and our circumstances as either a total success or a total failure. Having burnout does not mean that we are failures. So, to counteract this, think back over the situation that led to burnout and salvage all the positives from it. This might be looking back over a professional or caring life. Ask yourself:

- What did I enjoy about my life then?

- Who did I meet whose companionship was good?

- What did I achieve?

- What am I proud of? What qualities did I show?

- What valuable memories do I have?

Build up a list of the good aspects of your previous situation and record them. Write them in your journal. It might even be right to celebrate your time before burnout with a special meal. It may feel a little like a requiem, and it may be one. But such things have a place in helping us appreciate memories we will always have that no one can take away.

WHAT CAN BE SALVAGED FROM THE WRECKAGE?

Our lives might have been shipwrecked but our survival may depend on us rescuing as much good as we can from the wreckage and building it into our new lives. After a car crash, the first thing we do is to check and see how much damage has been done. Can we breathe? Can we move? Can we walk? And so, after burnout, it is helpful to do the same and count all the good that is left.

- You are still alive. That is no small thing. Some people literally work themselves to death or commit suicide in burnout.

- Take stock of all the good health that is left. Can you still exercise? Have you an appetite? Can you sleep at night? Can you make love to your partner?

- Are you able to engage with your other loved ones, your children, your parents, your friends?

- Can you get up in the morning?

- Can you concentrate on things? You must be able to concentrate a bit to read the words you are reading now!

- What energy do you have? You have enough energy left to want to recover, because you have bothered to pick up this book and read it.

You might like to take it further than just making a list; perhaps write a letter of thanks. The letter might be to God or your partner or whoever, and it will appreciate the fact that you have now stopped living the crazy life you were living before. You might like to paint a picture or make a model.

LEARNING THE LESSONS

Having carried out these assessments of the good that has been retained despite burnout, turn to looking back at what went wrong and begin to learn from previous mistakes. There are lots of different ways to start doing this but, overall, try to regard it as a positive thing. Remember, burnout gives a great opportunity to live life better than before, so this exercise is a key component in making the best of this chance. If we can spot where we went wrong, we can avoid doing so again in the future and plan for a better, more balanced life from here on.

Here are some suggested starting points. Pick the one that most appeals to you, then move on. In all of these suggested methods, or in any others, the main questions to try to answer are:

- What choices did I make throughout the process of becoming burnt out?

- Could I have acted differently, and if so, how?

- What were the messages I was giving myself that took me so far down the line? (For example, "I must not fail", "I must keep up with everybody else" and so on.)

- What messages am I giving myself now that I am burnt out and have admitted it? Are they positive or negative? Need I agree with them?

- What would I say as the person I am now to the person who was acting like that? What advice would I give? What message can I give to myself now? What lessons do I want to learn for the future?

Draw a timeline

This can be just about your burnout and can begin with when you think the burnout began or earlier, perhaps going back to the beginning of your time of employment or even further back. It needn't be all neat on a piece of A4 or on the screen of your computer. You might like to get a roll of lining paper and make the timeline quite big, writing with felt pens, and finish up with it Blu-Tacked to a wall. You could add pictures or photos to it.

- Begin by marking the obvious points, starting with employment, moving to different jobs, being sacked or disciplined, or when a new colleague arrived. Do that in one colour.

- Then go over it again with another colour, writing in more subjective points of time, such as when you began to lose interest in your work, when your burnout began, when you got tired and disillusioned.

- Plot in it particular incidents that stand out in your memory: the day of the meeting where you lost it, the time you had a row with your colleague, the time your boss doubled your workload when a colleague wasn't replaced, the time you began to bring work home for evenings and weekends, or started staying late in the office, or began a lot of overseas travel and so on. Mark them with a different coloured pen.

- Take a fourth colour that stands for your family life and for changes in your family circumstances. Plot in your start in life, your birth, childhood and adolescence, noting the major highs and lows. Then move on to your adult life, doing the same. Note the pattern of your early adult life. Were there significant relationships? Did you have children? Did you have to start caring for an elderly relative? Note then when the pressure began to build: when you had to see less of your family in order to make room for work, when there was trouble about something in the family, when your partner, if you had one, began to show signs of being unhappy with the present arrangements, when there was illness in the family, whether, if you were alone, it was the isolation which helped fuel the burnout – or whatever applies to you.

- Then take a fifth colour. This stands for your social life: interests, sports or other clubs, garden, outdoor pursuits, local church or place of worship, whatever it is. Plot them in the timeline as well. We would expect involvement in these to drop off the longer and deeper your problem with burnout proved to be, but not necessarily so.

When the timeline is done, have a look at it. Do the different colours form a pattern? What sort of story do they tell you?

You may also want to get your partner or a trusted friend to look at the timeline and see what they think. You want to draw significant things on it. Put a big arrow where things began to go wrong, write a motto where there is room, and decide what you would want to avoid in the future.

Write the story out

As mentioned in the previous chapter, writing has an illuminating effect in all kinds of stress, including burnout. Writing clarifies things: we realize as we write what was going on. So try writing out the story of your burnout.

- Begin where you like, letting your pen or keyboard take you where it will. Don't worry if it seems rambling or incoherent, or if your English isn't great; just write. The great thing about writing therapeutically is that you can't write the wrong thing. Everything you write will be helpful. Be aware that there may well be some resistance to starting to do this, but do it anyway.

- Only write for twenty minutes at the most – less if you become exhausted.

- When it is written, put it away for at least a week, maybe longer. Don't be tempted to go back over it. If you have written it in more than one sitting, you shouldn't reread before you start to write again. Nor should you pore over it when you have finished a session, but get up and do something else and then come back to it later and, when it is over, put it away.

- After a week or so, take it out and read it through and note down what it makes you feel. Again, you don't have to write great prose or poetry – it might be no more than a list of emotions. Don't worry if your writing gets quite pungent and isn't fit to be shown to anybody else. Don't be shocked. Let those feelings come onto the page. Don't worry about writing powerful, violent things about people who have hurt you; let them come onto the page as well. Then, when you have written all you feel you want to, put it away. Don't keep going over it. Forget it as best you can.

Probably after two or three goes, you will find that your feelings have cooled, your head has cleared, and you are able to write more about the decisions that were taken, and how much choice you had or didn't have. Keep writing, ideally until you feel you can see more clearly how things went wrong.

Then write a final piece entitled "What went wrong? What could I have done differently and what do I intend to do in the future?"

The cucumber theory: taking a critical incident in your story

Wherever you cut a cucumber, the pattern of the seeds is the same. Some people believe that you can take just one incident out of somebody's life from more or less anywhere in their story, young, middle-aged or old, and look at the patterns, and they will tell you the story of the person. Certainly it is likely that taking a particular incident in your burnout story and analysing it closely will tell you things about how the burnout happened and what sort of decisions you were taking at that time.

To choose your critical incident, by which we mean an incident that stands out strongly, we suggest using the float-back method.

The float-back method

Take a quiet moment or so, sit back in your chair, don't force your memory but let the whole history of what happened float back over you, a bit like the landscape running by as you sit on a train. Let your story run by and then, just like on a railway journey, a particular tree or pylon might stand out, so let your memory free fall and focus on a particular time. The one you choose might come as a surprise; it wouldn't be one that you'd have picked if you'd tried to think of it in some other way. But go with it; it's likely to be more significant than you might think. Or, you may find you pick a memory that has stayed with you very strongly all through.

Once you have selected your memory, we suggest working on it on this model. Again it is best to write things down rather than just do it mentally.

- Describe the incident; write down what happened. Don't interpret or read in any emotion; just write a bare factual account as if you were a police officer writing something up for the court.

- Describe what emotions you were feeling as the incident took place. Are they anger, humiliation, fear, anxiety, shock? There are many to choose from.

- Write down an answer to the question, "What did this incident make me feel about myself? What conclusions about my circumstances and myself as a person did I draw?" This might be, "I was useless… weak… was outmanoeuvred… a failure."

- Consider what evidence you are using to draw this conclusion. What part of the story are you using to decide that you were weak or ineffectual or whatever?

- Need this be the case? Is there an alternative inference that could be drawn on the same evidence? For instance, "I had no choice. I was caught between getting away from the pressure and leaving the job, or being able to pay the mortgage and feed my family."

- If you draw another conclusion, how does that leave you feeling about yourself in the incident? And here maybe "I was weak" or "I was guilty" or "I was to blame" or "I was a failure" might change to something nearer the truth, which might be "I was a victim of circumstance; I had tried very hard over many years to serve the organization I worked in, but at this point the demands became too strong". As you look at the incident you might want to think about what you would say to yourself now.

- Decide what lessons you can learn from the incident, and if it were to happen to you again, what you might do. But also think about how to avoid it happening again.

Working in this way is very similar to Cognitive Behavioural Therapy, a form of treatment that encourages us to ask questions about the way we think about ourselves and our underlying assumptions. If you want to look into this more, there are several websites that give a good introduction to CBT and a taster of it, which we mention in the Resources section.

Talking it through with another person
At some stage in your burnout, you will have lost the ability to hear other people very clearly. You will have started to blank out other people's voices, and also have lost the capacity to hear what you were saying to yourself and what was happening within you. Making contact with another person at a time of burnout can be a really helpful way to get clear about what has gone on. It is important to make a conscious decision to listen to what they say, even if you don't feel able to agree with it.

Take care who you talk to, and how and when you talk to them. We write in Chapter 10 about the pros and cons of talking with family members, friends and different sorts of professionals. You might like to jump ahead and read that now, or you may prefer to wait.

IN CONCLUSION

Finally, you may not want to use any of the methods suggested, and there are other ways of doing things. You might like to write fiction, to work through artwork – drawing, painting, sculpture or modelling. As always, when working with yourself following burnout, please be gentle. Take time. Don't force the pace. If you try these things and find you just can't do them, then wait until you have enough energy.

Our bodies and psyches have within them the capacity to cure themselves over time, if they are allowed that time and space, so don't be in a rush. Wait until there is some desire and enthusiasm within you for trying things out and, when you do begin, don't be too hard on yourself for the mistakes you have made. They were probably very understandable mistakes, made under pressure, and you may not have had that much choice. In so far as you were at fault, it is in the past now and no good can come from beating yourself up about this any more. The only good that can come is by learning the lessons and trying not to repeat any mistakes in the future.

Remember, having become burnt out is a great opportunity. It's a chance to do things differently in the future. Working on the past can lead to a happy and fulfilled life ahead of you, better than the one you have lived so far.

PART THREE

. . . .

Part Three of this book is designed to cover many different areas of life where burnout is likely to have affected you, by robbing you of their particular value. They are all important. A healthy person will have an interest in all of them to some extent. As you recover from burnout we offer these various areas to consider. As you rebuild your life and reconsider your values, wanting to make sure you do not burn out again, we think looking at them and entering into at least some of them will be formative in having a healthier, more balanced outlook so you can start to enjoy life again. There is quite a lot of material here, so do please go easy on yourself. Just follow up the ones that seem the most relevant at first, because they can be read in any order. The final chapter draws it all together and suggests ways you can work on an overall plan to re-enter normal life, free of the danger of any more burnout.

9

How Can I Mend My
Relationships?

Addressing broken relationships can be vital to making a recovery from burnout. It would be unusual to experience burnout and not have gone through difficult relationships. In our work with burnout sufferers, we have found that difficult or damaged personal relationships stand out for people the most. This may be about people who treat us badly: business colleagues or demanding relatives. It might even be those we do not really relate to at all, such as high-up executives in a multinational organization based in a different continent whose decisions have wrecked our lives, or government ministers responsible for policies that have affected us adversely. Or maybe they are members of the general public, whose ingratitude or indifference has worn us down.

Richard says, "I was undermined by my employers, who were unwilling to engage with the structural issues that were hindering me from doing my job, and which led to burnout." He believes his burnout resulted from dysfunctional work arrangements and lack of basic support from senior people in the church who handled him incompetently and seemed to be in denial about what had occurred. Lily also had issues with her employers: she lost her sense of fulfilment at work when two new bosses were appointed over her head, and she found she could not respect them. The job was otherwise the same, but her deteriorating relationships drew her into burnout.

There is often a complex web of blame around burnout, and work needs to be done to ascertain how much is our own fault and how much is the fault of others. Once we have identified, even roughly, where fault lies, we need to be reconciled in these relationships, in so far as we can, so we can get on with our lives.

Heather's story is of an otherwise able and contented senior teacher burning out through a bad relationship with her new head teacher.

....

Interview: Heather

Heather is a retired teacher, who worked in a pupil referral unit with children and young people who had been excluded from mainstream schools. She writes:

I am passionate about teaching, creative, outgoing and innovative, and I frequently worked long hours seeking the best for the children. When I was fifty-nine the pressure at work intensified when an ineffective and incompetent head teacher was appointed to my unit. Towards the end of an exhausting term, in the middle of an Ofsted inspection and in front of others, I was abruptly asked to go home by the head with no explanation given.

I was already exhausted through hard work. My husband had been asking me to spend less time on [it]. My children described me as obsessive about work, and told me I could think and talk of nothing else. The shock of the way I had been treated at school resulted in me becoming tearful, unable to eat or sleep and complaining of aches and pains. I lost my confidence in several areas and found reading or computer work very difficult. I went to my GP, who put me on extended sick leave and suggested I see a counsellor. I had six sessions of counselling which were very useful. It helped me to see that I had nothing to blame myself for. I was shown how to take control of my situation, recognizing what had happened and not simply accepting the situation but choosing what to do about it. I also found walking and going to rugby matches therapeutic.

My husband was a tremendous support to me, and saw it as an opportunity for me to recover from my exhaustion. My family and many of my friends were also a great [help]. I didn't get much support from work. I did contact my union representative who offered me advice and support in meetings. My previous head teacher was extremely helpful. I contacted her immediately after the incident, and another teaching friend phoned me regularly and would not let me blame myself. My [Christian] faith was a major source of strength and helped me keep going.

I never returned to work but was on sick leave until my retirement at age sixty. I find a slower pace of life suits me now. If I had been younger I would have taken out a grievance procedure against the head but was too exhausted to contemplate it. I have since been able to offer support to other colleagues in similar situations.

Very frequently, becoming burnt out will have affected our close relationships. For some people, burnout has involved a divorce or separation; others are aware that there has been a strain on their marriage or partnership. Then, of course, there are other close relationships with children, parents and friends.

There was once a full-page advert in a daily paper which showed a young man with his bride on the steps of the church. Everything was what you'd expect. There was the church building, there was him in his morning suit, there were guests throwing confetti, there was a photographer, there were bridesmaids, there was a bride in a beautiful white dress. The only difference was that the bride was not a woman but a middle-aged man, and the caption on the advert was "Are you married to the boss?" We forget just what the advert was selling but that powerful image has stayed with us. Often in workplace burnout scenarios we may as well have been married to the boss, because they have had the lion's share of our time, energy, commitment and even love. We have put our other relationships on hold and taken for granted those around us who are close to us. This can be equally true where burnout stems not from the workplace but from a need to offer long-term care. This can have a detrimental effect on our other relationships. So this chapter is about restoring our relationships. You may come to almost bless the day you burnt out, and see it as the time when you came to your senses and realized just who was important to you – and who was not.

Just about all the books on burnout we consulted stress the vital importance of guarding our close relationships. Bruce and Katherine Epperly, in their book *Feed the Fire,* dedicate a chapter to the subject. They say, "We are profoundly relational… we find wholeness, vitality and fulfilment in healthy relationships, whether in a committed lifelong relationship or through faithful friends. Relationships bring healing and wholeness."[1]

Either, through overwork, personal relationships have been sacrificed and put under too much strain, putting severe pressure on family life, or it was difficult relationships which were the main cause of the burnout and thus stay most potently in the memory during burnout. Or both may be true. So we might need to do *restoration work* where we have neglected relationships and *reconciliation work* where we feel we have been hurt by others.

Here are some simple ideas about mending our relationships. We do want to acknowledge before we start that relationships are complex, sensitive things. Mending them needs care and we will often make mistakes. Nonetheless, if our intentions are good, that will shine through.

RESTORATION

First, we suggest some sort of assessment is made of the present situation. What state are your close relationships in now?

- Are you married or in a stable loving partnership?

- How would you describe the nature of this relationship at this moment?

- Do you still live with any dependent children?

- What are their current needs?

- What is the current state of your relationship with them?

- What is the current state of your relationship with your parents, or any siblings?

- Do these relationships need input?

- What about your friends?

Mapping exercise

The first exercise we suggest at this point is the simple one of listing those with whom you are in relationship and giving a mark out of 10 for how much you think they have been affected by your burnout. A score of 10 would indicate a total disruption of your relationship and a score of 0 would mean they are totally unaffected by your burnout.

Having completed the list of your relationships, take your time reviewing it. How many of them have scored 5 or over? Try repeating this exercise in a few days' time, to see if you still think the same. You may have begun by underestimating the effect of your burnout on your loved ones. Further thought may lead you to think differently.

Now, move on to what needs to be done if these relationships are to be restored. Take a single sheet of paper or a page in your journal for each of your relationships which have scored 3 or above in the earlier part of the exercise. On it, try to give as honest answers as you can to the questions set out below. These are basic questions designed to help you decide what you might do to restore any lost love and intimacy with those close to you.

Name ....

1. What is there that is still good about my relationship with them?

2. How have they been affected by my burnout?

3. What emotions are they likely to be feeling towards me right now?

4. What would they say to me if they really spoke their minds?

5. Do I need to apologize to them for the way burnout has caused me to behave?

6. If I do, how, when and where is it best to make this apology?

7. What else can I do to improve things?

8. What would be the best way to reach out to them?

9. In what order would it be best to start restoring this relationship?

10. What should be the first move?

11. Do we both need time before I do anything explicit?

Once you have written answers for the people with whom you are in relationship, then put them into practice. It is difficult for us to give specific guidance beyond this point because so much will depend upon the particular circumstances, but here are a few helpful pointers:

Least said soonest mended. It might simply be that as you are changing your attitudes to yourself, being less hard on yourself and giving yourself proper care and space, you begin to do this with your nearest and dearest as well. They will then begin to feel properly valued and loved. Wounded relationships may begin to be healed without a great deal needing to be said.

Actions speak louder than words. What your family will be looking for will be actual changes in your behaviour. This will matter to them much more than any fine words, however sincere they are. So it is worth thinking about what you can do which will mend relationships every bit as much as what you can say. And it's doing it over time. There may be further slip-ups, but if you carry on doing good things towards your loved ones, that will win them back.

Apologize and listen. Nonetheless, words are very important. And it may well be that it is appropriate to say something to restore relationship. Here are a few tips. Keep it short. Keep it simple. Apologize for what you know to have been wrong. Don't give excuses. Don't justify yourself. Don't promise the earth by way of your future behaviour; no one becomes a saint overnight – just promise to do your best to be different in the future. End by offering to listen to what they want to say back. And then make sure you do listen to what they say back. Give them space; they have suffered much pain. Just keep attentive, focused and listening. Don't interrupt. Don't argue. Just stay there. Aim at doing at least twice as much listening as talking. Plan time for that.

Don't forget our old friend – writing. Write out beforehand what you want to say. It will sharpen your mind, and it might be better put in a letter. It will also show forethought, planning and earnestness, though it carries the danger of seeming distant. A compromise on this is to hand your letter over for your loved one to read while you stay there. It may even work well to read it out to them, though it might seem somewhat stylized.

Don't rush or try to sort out everything and everyone all at once. Take your time. Better done a little later with proper forethought than rushed.

It may go wrong anyway! When you love people, it can all come out wrong, and not as you planned. Don't worry. If you love them and they love you, they will read your heart, not your mind. They will understand sooner or later. They will forgive you. You will laugh about it later. What they want is you, healthy and properly loving them as they deserve.

RECONCILIATION

In this section we think about the hurts that have been done to us, and maybe also the things we have done to others in our working situation.

Mapping exercise

As with our work on restoration, it is good to do a mapping exercise to begin with. Create a list of characters that were involved in bringing you to burnout. Its length will probably surprise you. Here's a suggested list of people who may well be involved in a work burnout situation:

- your immediate boss

- their boss

- all the bosses up to the top
- your peers – colleagues at your level
- those colleagues under you whose boss you were
- members of other rival firms or institutions
- customers, clientele, patients, etc.

In the case of minors, if you have been in charge of them:

- their parents
- government and government policy
- economic factors, the recession
- the people responsible for it
- family pressure
- family expectations
- the general public.

You may well be able to add to this list. So now you have a list of characters that have hurt you and brought about the burnout. The next part of the exercise is to put them in order of weight of offence. Put those who have offended you the most at the top, and those who have offended least at the bottom. Take your time. It might surprise you. For instance, if you are a teacher, the two main people who have caused your burnout might be as different as the Minister of Education in the cabinet and Tommy Jones in Year 10 who made your life such a constant misery.

Choosing who to work on
Having got your prioritized list of characters, make a choice as to which you will work on. It may not be the ones at the top of

the list. Their offence might be so raw and powerful that you aren't yet in a place even to address some form of reconciliation. You would be better looking at which ones on the list seem the most manageable, which ones you could cope with. There may not be any! If so, leave it a while longer. However, there is also the danger of procrastination, avoiding conflict when your best recovery from burnout would be to take on some attempt at reconciliation. So, make a judgement.

If you do decide to try to work for reconciliation, then here are some pointers as to how to go about it.

Possible methods of reconciliation

1. Direct formal action
It may be that your circumstances justify some sort of direct approach to those who have caused you harm. This may be legal and formal, such as an employment tribunal or a grievance procedure for unfair dismissal, or some form of hard-edged negotiation for a decent financial settlement and a reference carried out through lawyers. This book does not set out to advise about any kind of legal process, but we do suggest getting proper legal advice before proceeding. These things are time-consuming and costly in terms of money, time and energy, and it is important to know whether it is going to be worth your while undertaking them. They are often harrowing to go through and it would be important to have good support not only in terms of legal advice, but emotionally from family and friends and maybe a professional source as well.

As we have seen, Heather considered going down this route but decided not to. That is a valid decision.

2. Meeting up
It might be possible to actually meet up with somebody who has behaved badly towards you and have some kind of active reconciliation with them. The reconciling effect of just

meeting in the flesh is amazing, even if the conversation is unsatisfactory. It might be as informal as meeting up for a drink (neutral venues help), or it may be more formal, such as using a mediation service that specializes in bringing together people in serious dispute. In the case of criminal hurt, the police sometimes arrange for victims and offenders to meet, or at least exchange letters. Even if you can't meet in the flesh, you can pretend. Try placing an empty chair opposite you. Imagine the person is sat in the chair. Tell them exactly what you think of them, even in their absence. It can sometimes be helpful to put something such as a cushion or a symbol of them on the chair.

3. No-send letters
Direct action or meeting up may not be appropriate, and indeed, in some instances, would never be appropriate (e.g. pupils in a former school). In such a case, try a "no-send letter". Write out in the form of a letter just what you think about what they have done and what you think about them as people. It's called a no-send letter because the intention is that it will not be posted. Knowing that, you can write just what you feel. Don't worry if it is explosive stuff. Don't worry if it is full of expletives and hot emotions. Let it come out. Later, it might be right to edit it into something that is sent, and there may be benefit in sending it, but in its no-send form, it still does a lot of good as a cathartic way to get your feelings out, and also to come to terms with what has happened to you. As we have already explained, writing things out can be good for us, and this is true of no-send letters.

4. Some sort of dramatic or external act
It can be helpful sometimes to go through an act which externalizes or brings to a dramatic conclusion your involvement with a hurtful set of people or circumstances. In the film *South Pacific*, the heroine sings, "I'm gonna wash that man right outa

my hair"; by the act of washing her hair she feels she is getting rid of a bad relationship. The kind of things we have in mind might include:

- burning the no-send letter

- having a celebration meal, to draw a line under your time of pain

- burying a symbolic object, a bit like the Red Indians buried the hatchet to make peace, or just getting rid of things associated with a former situation – papers from a job, or the clothes for that job, or something similar

- doing something aggressive such as hitting a punchbag or just getting on your own somewhere out of earshot, screaming and shouting out all the feelings that are inside.

5. Exploring forgiveness

Forgiveness is about simply letting someone off the offences they have done to us. It's not easy but it is possible. If this area is of interest, we suggest as a first step a visit to the website of The Forgiveness Project, whose address is in the Resources section at the end of this book. It was started by people who were badly hurt during the troubles in Ulster and has now become a worldwide movement. If you visit the pages of the website where people tell their stories, you may well be inspired by what can be achieved when people will embrace forgiveness after being hurt.

Ultimately, if we are to have a healthy outlook, whether in burnout or not, we need to forgive those who have hurt us and seek forgiveness where we have hurt others. We are surprised how little the concept of forgiveness is used in the therapeutic world. It plays a large part in both world politics and the major faiths. And there is the further dimension of forgiving ourselves. It may be that a refusal to forgive ourselves was part of our burnout. Dina Glouberman says:

> *Another benefit of forgiveness is that it reassures us*
> *on a deep level that nothing is unforgiveable. What*
> *drove us forward ... towards burnout was that if*
> *we stopped doing or being, achieving whatever it*
> *was, we would be worthless, wicked, selfish, bad. We*
> *would not be forgiven. By forgiving we tell ourselves*
> *now and forever that nothing is unforgiveable.*[2]

6. Consideration of those worse off than ourselves

People often take great comfort from the fact that there is always somebody worse off than themselves – and with good reason. Again, we suspect that if we have looked up the stories on the web pages of The Forgiveness Project we will have been overwhelmed by a sense of how deep people's sufferings are compared to our own. The stories of imprisonment, violence, multiple rape and much else that has happened to people all round the world will hopefully put our own sufferings, bad as they are, into perspective. If we have suffered similarly in any way, we will see that we are not alone and that it is possible to move forward.

7. Advocacy against the injustices that have harmed us

It might be possible that through what we have suffered in our burnout, we might be able to be an advocate to prevent it happening to anybody else. This could be true in a variety of settings: industry, care, or a voluntary organization. We might consider writing to any governing bodies these organizations have, or joining an association or a support group for people who have suffered in a similar way to us. Becoming an advocate, apart from its intrinsic worth, helps us because we feel something constructive has come out of what has been a negative experience. If we are able to do some good as a result of what has harmed us, this in itself helps us to be reconciled to what has happened to us.

A final footnote

In the matter of reconciliation overall, it is always worth trying to put ourselves inside the skin of the person who has hurt us. Imagine you were them; imagine the pressures you know or think they were under. Probably you will still feel they acted badly, and that you would not have done the same in their shoes, but you may be able to see a little at least of where they were coming from. Imagine what view of you they may have held – were you a threat to them, were you another burden to them on top of all else that they were suffering? Think of what you know about their personal circumstances – were they ill, did they have other troubles in their personal lives? What sort of pressures might they have been under professionally? Often when we are put under undue pressure at work by a boss, it's because they themselves are under similar pressure from those above them.

Trying to think in this way may help you to be reconciled to what has taken place in your own life.

10

How Can I Know *Myself Better?*

Another important phase in coming out of burnout is to do some work on ourselves. There is great truth in the Shakespearean phrase "To thine own self be true",[1] but if we don't really know much about ourselves that can be difficult. This chapter is designed to help you look at your natural self, your talents and abilities and the choices you have made so far. We give advice on how to consider the potential choices that lie ahead, with a view to restarting active working life in a way most suited to your personality, and hence the most fruitful and least stressful. You need to be realistic about what you can manage to do well, rather than comparing that with what you feel you should be able to do, or what you used to do, or what someone else can do.

Justin and Margaret mentioned understanding themselves better as an important factor in recovering from stress and burnout. Margaret thinks it is very important to look at your lifestyle and make changes where needed. She says, "It's important to recognize your personality type too – I am someone who is ambitious, sets goals and pushes myself hard to achieve them. In times past I... ignored my body's warning signs that it (and in fact nobody) could keep up with what I was asking."

Justin's experience of severe stress when he was a deputy head made him more self-aware and less ambitious. He says, "My priorities changed ... I made the decision to change my lifestyle at age fifty, so making the high-pressure job time-limited. [Then] I took a less demanding job outside of teaching, working for a charity. This job made use of my skills in organizing and motivating people, satisfied my love of travel, and gave me job satisfaction."

So how can you begin to know and understand yourself? You may know a great deal already, but all too often it is hard to give the time and space needed to really thinking about what you know. There are several routes to learning and understanding more about yourself. In so doing, you may begin to appreciate just why you drive yourself so hard, and just what deep inner need or desire is being satisfied in the process.

PERSONALITY INDICATORS

Personality indicators are useful tools to help people understand themselves, and give good insights. We give a selection of recommended personality indicators in the Resources section. The most widely recognized one with which we are the most familiar is the Myers-Briggs Type Indicator (MBTI), a self-report questionnaire designed to make Jung's theory of psychological types understandable and useful in everyday life. Katharine Briggs and her daughter, Isabel Briggs Myers, were two American women who observed people, elaborated Jung's ideas, and developed the Indicator. The MBTI is well researched and the most widely used instrument for understanding personality differences. It greatly enhances self-understanding.

It is based on preferences, with no right or wrong answers. It has four dimensions, reflecting our preferred ways of:

- making decisions
- getting energy
- taking in information
- dealing with the world.

For example, although we could use either hand to write with, we prefer to use either the right or the left, feeling more comfortable with one and using it unconsciously for preference. We would say we are right- or left-handed, although most of us use our non-preferred hand for a number of other things, and if we lost the use of our preferred hand, we could train ourselves to use our other hand. Similarly we will have a preference about many ways of behaving. We may be able to be very organized and systematic in certain situations (perhaps in our job), but we actually prefer to be casual and flexible, and that feels most natural to us. Or vice versa: we train ourselves to go with the flow but left to ourselves we would prefer to be systematic. The MBTI helps us to understand what our natural preferences are, and gives us a "type". There are sixteen different "types", all with their particular strengths and weaknesses.

It may be that the job we are working in does not altogether match our individual preferred way of being, and that we have to act in a way that doesn't feel natural when we are in our work role. People get the most satisfaction from careers that provide them with opportunities to express and use their preferred type. We may, for instance, have difficulties with individuals in our workplace because their preferred mode of operating is opposite to our own. If our preferred way of making decisions is analytical, logical problem-solving, we may appear callous to those who prefer to make decisions based on how others will be affected. Do we prefer to avoid last-minute stress or are we energized into action by it? This type of question will be answered by the

MBTI. It is great fun to do, and often very liberating too, as we begin to understand why we and others around us act in a certain way. The MBTI can be done either online or by participation in workshops, as can most other personality indicators.

TALKING WITH A PARTNER OR GOOD FRIEND

We have briefly discussed the value of talking things through with those close to us in Chapter 8. It has the great advantage that they know us the best and will want the best for us. Our understanding of who we are and what we are like often comes through our interaction with others. We see ourselves reflected back to us by those around us. So it can be very helpful in trying to understand ourselves to talk with our family and friends and listen to what they say about us.

Talking things through with your partner or a close family member will bring many benefits. They will know you like no other, and often will have done so for many years. They love you, they may have sacrificed for you and they will only want the best for you. At the same time, the disadvantage of help and advice from close family is that it is inevitably coloured by those very same things. They may live emotionally very close to you – too close to keep a distant enough perspective. Despite themselves, they will know that their fate is bound up with yours, and what they offer you by way of advice can't help but be affected by that. So although wise advice and reflection from a partner or family member is invaluable, it can be flawed and needs to have other advice alongside it too.

Trusted friends are good to talk to as well. They care about you. They will have been concerned to see you burn out. They can be candid and are not bound into your immediate circumstances in the way your family will be. They obviously like you in order to have stayed your friend and may know you very well. They may have known you from a young age, even as a child, and so have seen you grow and develop. They can be more detached than your own kith and kin, so their advice and feedback is very helpful too.

When talking with them, we suggest doing so more formally than just having a casual chat over coffee or a pint in the pub. Ask your friends to take some trouble over both listening to you and offering any perspectives. It might be best to ask them to work on paper, with you writing things down for them and them replying.

There are some disadvantages in talking with friends too. They probably won't have professional skills in listening and counselling. At the same time they will not be able to be truly detached precisely because they are your friends. They may feel inhibited in challenging you, for fear of spoiling a long-lasting friendship or making the situation worse. And it has to be faced that with family, partners and friends, there is a certain boredom threshold. When we are hurt, we tend to talk repeatedly about our wounds. We also stubbornly don't get better all that quickly. You are not the same as you used to be because you are burnt out and your existing family and friends have to adjust to that loss of the past, just as you do. They are not being paid to listen and may quite quickly reach a place of feeling listening to you is too much of a burden, even if they don't show it. Listening to people undergoing serious emotional distress is emotionally taxing in itself.

You, in talking to them, and they in replying, will be prone to censor what is said. It would be unusual for you not to feel rather embarrassed and ashamed about your burnout, which may cause you to be careful what you say to them. They may also, despite themselves, have felt in competition with you through the years. This is far from unusual in friendships and may skew what they have to say. There may be very personal elements as well in your circumstances that you simply can't share with them. So it is really important to choose carefully which friends you talk to.

Margaret had a lot of support from her close family, and at work they were understanding. About her friendships she says, "[They] were severely challenged... some friends didn't understand what was happening, but others were supportive."

TALKING IT THROUGH WITH A LOCAL PROFESSIONAL (GP, LAWYER, UNION REPRESENTATIVE, MINISTER)

There is much to be said for talking to local professionals. They may know you quite well, and will have expertise in advising a cross-section of people. They will be detached, and will specialize in certain areas, which could also be helpful.

Several of our interviewees talked things through with professionals: Ross went to a lawyer, because he believed he had been unfairly dismissed, and also discussed what had led to his burnout with his GP and local vicar. Clare talked things through with the occupational health department at work and was offered the opportunity of working part-time, while Nicola needed to see her doctor and received some medication, but also the opportunity to return to work part-time when she was able.

ENGAGING PROFESSIONAL HELP

We would strongly suggest considering therapy from someone who is professionally qualified. They will have been trained to listen empathically and not to judge, and also to reflect back what they have heard their clients say. We are both therapists and we may be biased, but in our experience, people can be radically helped just by the simple business of taking focused time with a professional to talk through their issues. Often a lot of new things come to light and people usually go away feeling very glad they have entered therapy, and with a much deeper understanding of themselves.

There are three types of professional help you might consider. They are:

- therapists/counsellors

- cognitive behavioural specialists

- other professional advisors.

Therapists/counsellors

There is still a lot of stigma attached to seeing a therapist or counsellor, though this is lessening. A recent survey showed that one in five of all Britons has consulted a counsellor or psychotherapist and that 94 per cent now consider it acceptable to have counselling. Really, counselling is only an extension of the time-honoured instinct to share with a stranger. When we are under strain, we often end up pouring it all out to someone we meet on the train or in a bar. The fact that they are removed from our circle helps us feel free to unburden. Counselling offers this same detachment from our existing relationships but adds in the vital elements of training and professional standards.

A good therapist will principally listen, offering space in which to express the issues. This in itself is immensely valuable; so much so that there is a specialty within the counselling world of "non-directive" counselling, which is virtually entirely confined to listening. But most counsellors will in addition to listening offer reflections on what they have heard, and work with their clients in some way to help them understand themselves better.

There are three conventional orientations within counselling.

- **Humanistic counselling.** This where the counsellor offers person-to-person human contact as their main way of effecting change. The human qualities of empathy, acceptance and care are understood to create a good space for the client to work out their own issues.

- **Psychodynamic counselling.** This is where the work is concentrated on the client's past, looking for learned patterns of behaviour which are still affecting the present.

- **Behavioural counselling.** This begins with the present problem and works at alleviating it, to make it manageable. Then further work is done to look at the underlying assumptions which made the client behave harmfully to themselves. Once these come to light, work is done to seek to change them.

The three orientations are not mutually exclusive and most counsellors integrate all three methods of working.

People fear counselling is expensive and time-consuming. In fact, nowadays counselling is readily available on the NHS. Most GP surgeries offer it, though waiting lists can run to some months. In the private market the average cost of a counselling session is about £45 per hourly session and the average frequency is an hour a week. This is a significant amount of money, though appreciably less than the cost of a tank of petrol for the average family car. There are many counselling services which offer discretionary rates or sliding scales for payment. As therapists we feel this commitment of time and money is well worth it, to get to grips with the major issues which have come close to wrecking lives through burnout.

Examples

Heather's GP suggested that she see a counsellor. She says, "I had six sessions with him which really helped. He made me understand that I had nothing to blame myself for, and that I had to take control of my situation. The following advice from the counsellor to say to myself was very helpful: 'I have done nothing wrong. I am not to blame. I will be merciful to myself and others. I will treat myself. This is the way it is; I look ahead to the future. I don't simply accept it, which is passive, I choose it, which is proactive.'"

As he said in his story, John talked to his boss and was referred to a stress counsellor, which he found extremely helpful. He says they made a number of useful suggestions which he put into practice, such as drinking plenty of water, keeping a notebook by his bed for when he couldn't sleep, and taking up cooking for himself and not simply buying ready meals.

Cognitive behavioural specialists

Cognitive Behavioural Therapy (CBT) is the branch of therapy most strongly recommended for speedy changes of behaviour. It is the preferred option of the National Institute for Health and Clinical Excellence for mild depression and anxiety, phobias and compulsive disorders. We are including it here because we think that anyone with the standard symptoms of burnout would benefit from it too, and it helps us to understand our underlying system of beliefs about ourselves and the world, which affects the way we behave.

We all have negative underlying beliefs which affect the way we think. They are often deep underlying assumptions about life which have been there since our childhood, learned from the significant people in our lives. Common beliefs that can make us more vulnerable to burnout are encapsulated in such sentences as "I must never make a mistake" and "I can only be happy if I am totally successful". They do not cause us any trouble until something happens in our lives to challenge one of them. CBT will try to uncover some of the assumptions we make that are unhelpful and assist us in replacing them with alternative ways of seeing things. This is called cognitive restructuring.

How does CBT work? One of the basic goals of CBT is to get us to challenge negative thoughts by looking at all the information and evidence in our lives, then to evaluate the negative thoughts, and to think more helpfully.

Kate Middleton says, "Trying to suppress angry negative emotions is a bit like putting an angry cat in the box."[2]

When our mood is low, such as through burnout, we are more likely to interpret things negatively. We tend to maximize the bad and minimize the good. We are more likely to notice any negative aspects in our lives rather than positive or neutral ones. CBT helps us to learn to think more realistically. CBT reckons to get the cat out of the box and tame it. For example, say we are walking down the street and notice an old friend across the road. We get ready to greet them but they hurry by, with barely a glance at us. We may well, particularly if we are suffering from burnout or some other condition, jump to a negative conclusion about this. If we think "X didn't speak to me, they are ignoring me", we might begin to feel worried and go on to think other negative thoughts such as "I'm not worth bothering about, nobody likes me, I'm worthless, I may as well be dead".

CBT would challenge the negativity and explore more positive possibilities. For instance, we might think, "Poor X looked so worried. I wonder what has happened?" We would feel concern for them and we might phone later and ask how things are. This is a light hypothetical example, but CBT's real strength lies in looking at our overall negative assumptions about ourselves.

CBT is widely available through the NHS and privately. It particularly lends itself to self-help work. There are many useful self-help books that use CBT, the best known of which is *Clinician's Guide to Mind over Mood* (Christine A. Padesky and Dennis Greenberger, NY: Guilford Press, 1995), which has sold over 200,000 copies. There are good online CBT facilities too, The Mood Gym being the one we would most recommend. We give full details in the Resources section.

Other professional advisors

There are two other types of professional advisor we recommend using: life coaches and professional mentors.

Life coaches

Life coaching has grown out of counselling. It focuses more on people's life goals, their aims for the future. It may suit you better than counselling if you feel you have recovered from the worst effects of the burnout and are ready to decide what best to do in the future. According to Julia Bueno, life coaching

> *does not seek to resolve deeper underlying issues that can cause problems (like poor job performance/ self-esteem) but aims to set goals and achieve results within specific time-scales. Coaching is often seen as more positive, quicker, less painful and does not go into childhood, being less attached to the emotions.*[3]

We give the contact details of coaching bodies in the Resources section.

Professional mentors/consultants

The value of professional mentoring and consultancy is that it offers detailed expertise on the particular profession it deals with. We may need an expert opinion which is accurately informed about our own line of work – prospects for future employment, terms and conditions, recent developments which have happened while we have been away from the workplace and so on. These can only be obtained from someone who understands our area of expertise from the inside.

If you wish to re-enter your profession after a time away, or to enter a new one, then engaging a mentor or consultant whose work is to try to place people in a profession should be considered. They are trained to assess your experience and suitability for whatever type of work you are looking for. Also, they should have knowledge of the market and contacts within it to assist you in getting placed. Here there will be no personal work about the inner self at all. It will be a strictly profession-based process, and is well worth considering, alongside getting to know yourself in other ways.

The best way of learning more about yourself is to collect input from as many different places as possible, as Ed discovered – he attributes his recovery to consulting a wide variety of people, including his wife, friends and professional advisors.

11

What Can I Do About My Inner Emptiness?

When we suffer burnout, it shatters our beliefs about ourselves and the world. Our normal perspectives on life, which we have taken for granted, are turned upside down and we struggle to find meaning in what has happened to us. As we chronically overwork we may be left with a sense of inner emptiness and despair. The inner emptiness that accompanies burnout is very distressing, especially as we find that we tend to fall back on our inner reserves in times of stress.

A personal spirituality is now recognized as playing an important role in both emotional and psychological recovery. Donna Andronicos calls this "our innate desire to feel a sense of connection to something greater than ourselves; a feeling of belonging, peace of mind or awareness of a higher level of existence that goes beyond our normal physical and psychological being".[1]

D.C. Khakha, an Indian writer, says, "To enjoy a healthy, sustainable life, let your spirit be constantly renewed."[2] This chapter looks at this important area and suggests how we can begin to address it.

WHAT DO WE MEAN BY SPIRITUALITY?

Spirituality is a wider, more inclusive concept than religion, and is not tied to particular cultural beliefs or traditions. Spirituality is about:

- having a sense of meaning and purpose in our life, which gives it significance and helps us feel fulfilled

- having a sense of belonging

- having a sense of connection to other people, the world and something beyond ourselves

- having a sense of acceptance of ourselves, our successes and failures, and knowing how we fit into the world.

For each one of us, spirituality is a unique experience. Religious practices and beliefs are often the focus of our spirituality, but we can express it through many ways:

- being creative

- giving of ourselves in acts of compassion

- enjoying nature

- reading literature or poetry or philosophy

- maintaining good family relationships

- joining in activities which involve cooperation and trust

- listening/singing/making sacred music

- art appreciation

- retreats

- belonging to a faith tradition and taking part in worship services and symbolic practices.

Two quite contradictory things have been going on in Western society over the last fifty or sixty years. The first is that we have become increasingly secular and materialistic – we are "consumers". We measure our value in wealth and what it can buy and the status it can bring, rather than in spiritual values. The need to keep up a standard of living to which we have become accustomed, and on which our children depend, is a major motivator in driving us on in the workplace. It can often contribute to burnout.

Austin, whose full story starts Chapter 13, says, "Our lives are culturally linked to constant improvement. If we fail to improve then we are failing. Our culture perpetuates an attitude of constant improvement... Am I living in a life where my expectations (spiritually and practically) have been shaped into a method of arriving, rather than those of a journey with ups and downs?"

Alongside this has been a growing interest in many different forms of spirituality: New Age spirituality, the occult, nature worship, and a return to the pre-Christian paganism, among others. At the same time, world religions have come on the scene in a very big way. All our big cities now have sizeable populations from all the world's major religions. New places of worship – mosques, gurdwaras and Hindu temples – are springing up as people express their spirituality through religious faith.

We want to suggest using your experience of burnout to begin to explore the realm of spirituality. We believe that if someone loses the sense of something bigger and beyond themselves, it is a serious loss, and can create some of the problems leading to burnout and despair. Spending time developing our personal spirituality can increase our self-confidence and self-esteem. It can aid us in developing nurturing relationships with others and with the natural and supernatural world. Through it we can come to a new sense of meaning, peace of mind and hope for our future. Clare, a psychiatrist, says, "I felt very supported by my experience and my continued exploration of the spiritual side of my life. I felt strengthened and refreshed by meditation and prayer. I found that my spiritual beliefs helped me to live one day at a time. This, combined with the belief that I would get through and be able to act wisely, helped considerably."

HOW TO GET STARTED

- As a first exercise, we suggest taking your journal and writing down some thoughts in answer to the question "How would I describe my own spirituality?" Included in your answer would be your own story and what experience of spirituality you have had. This might be some formal experience in an organized religion, or it might be more informal and personal. Of course, you may have had both kinds. Have you ever had what you would call a spiritual experience? A sense of something in and beyond the natural world, something which touched the numinous within you, caused wonderment, made you want to commune with or worship something greater than yourself? If so, take time to write it down.

- Secondly, we suggest writing something down in answer to the question "Where would I like to go from here if I were to explore spirituality rather more?" Which part of the wide array of spirituality and faiths touches your own spirit the most, and what will you do next to explore it?

We make some suggestions below about taking the exploration of spirituality a bit further, and the different starting points.

1. A regular time of quiet for reflection or meditation or prayer

Reflection. Much spiritual and religious thought is based around our mortality. As a central part of their outlook, differing faiths and spiritual pathways offer reflection on the fact that we will all die sooner or later.

We suggest reflecting on your own mortality by trying one or more of these exercises. This is best done by writing your thoughts in your journal. (Ed found this particularly helpful and it changed his priorities in his life.) They seem quite shocking at first – thinking about our death! – but in fact help us express what we *really* want from life. If this doesn't appeal to you, just skip on to the next point.

(a) Write your own obituary. The point is to reflect on what you have done with your life so far, and what you would really like to do. What would you say about yourself? What do you feel you have achieved? Are there things you would like to have done which you have not yet accomplished, and would like to before you die?

(b) Write your own epitaph. What would you put on your gravestone? This exercise forces us to condense our thoughts about our life into just a few words – a couple of lines or so. When it is done, reflect on it. Is it satisfying? Are you content that it should be your epitaph? If you are not content, what would you like to have been able to say?

(c) Write a will. Not just one about your goods and chattels, but what you would like to leave behind as your legacy. What would you say to your spouse and children (if you have them) and those who are close to you? How does it leave you feeling?

Once you consider your mortality, are there things which you would like to get on with and get done before it catches up with you?

Meditation. We have written about this more fully in Chapter 7 on creating mental space. This would be a good time to reread that extract or look in the Resources section for guidance on how to meditate, and plan to incorporate this into a regular practice. Beth took up yoga as a form of relaxation, because she felt it had both physical and spiritual positive influences.

Prayer. Research and opinion polls indicate most people pray at some time, often when in deep need. Do you ever pray? If so, to whom? If you were to pray, who would you pray to? If you already are within a tradition where prayer is used, you may like to revive it if it has been at all neglected. Maybe visiting your local place of worship would be a good idea.

2. Reading and studying religious or spiritual material

Reading some of the great religious texts can be creative and broadening, as well as serving to combat your burnout and refresh you spiritually. It is no accident that the Koran, the Bible, and the Upanishads have been huge sellers for centuries. If you are not drawn to religious texts then you may want to read some philosophy, literature or poetry.

3. Making supportive friendships

Finding someone else who has similar spiritual or religious aims can be very helpful. It might be possible for you to seek out someone who would give you advice and mentor you in exploring your spirituality. There are people who train and specialize in spiritual accompaniment, helping people explore their spirituality. It may not need to be so formal a thing.

You may know someone who has a strong spirituality that you admire, and you could ask them for some guidance or advice. Many faiths have discussions and work in groups, and offer opportunities for people wanting to learn more about faith. Looking on the Internet, in the Yellow Pages or in local bookstores would be a good place to start.

4. Retreats

There has been a tremendous upsurge in people using retreat centres of various kinds as an antidote to the busyness of modern life. Television programmes have been made about ordinary people going on a silent retreat. Retreats can be directed, with somebody mentoring you through your time, or undirected, where you are free to do as you like. They are often held in traditional buildings and create a sanctuary of peace and solitude, offering time to think and reflect. There are retreat centres in the UK for all the major world faiths, and others besides which are not identified with any particular recognized religion. We give the contact details for a cross section of them in the Resources at the end of this book. It is quite possible to take a retreat of your own devising, without going to a designated retreat centre. Simply taking some time out to dwell on the kind of thing we have just suggested (reading, reflection, prayer), using the meditative techniques, would be a kind of retreat. This could be especially appropriate where time and/or finances prohibit going off to a retreat centre.

Michael found going on a led retreat really helped him: "I was alone, but there was community there that was very loving, giving me the space that I needed. The speaker had a combination of humour and honesty that was like a gift. I was able to laugh and cry during sessions. The retreat kick-started exercise such as walking, which became a pattern of my time off."

CONCLUSION

Giving regular time and space to nourish our personal spirituality will help replenish our inner life. We will find daily living becomes more meaningful. On the road to burnout we increasingly feel isolated and cut off from those around us. Of necessity we narrow our focus and become centred on what we want to accomplish and our personal survival. Reaching out beyond ourselves to others in our family and community and to a higher power reverses this trend and brings a sense of belonging and connectedness. With this can come a deep measure of recovery.

12

How Can I Relax Properly and Look After Myself?

When we are working so hard to keep going, and ignoring the physical signals of impending burnout, we can reach the stage of becoming physically ill. We may need to go to our doctor and get advice about our health. We also need to be aware that how we feel physically connects intimately with our sense of well-being, affecting our emotions, mood, energy levels and motivation.

Interview: Margaret

Margaret is forty and working in the design industry. We have already heard about her first episode of burnout at the age of sixteen.

The second episode at age twenty-two was more serious. At that time I had been working very hard on a placement year in the design industry, and was getting ready to go to South Africa. Once in South Africa I found I couldn't speak much, felt very low emotionally and was physically tired. I found company exhausting, and withdrew to recharge myself, but then felt isolated, detached and alone. I lost confidence and found even small challenges overwhelming. I was unable to handle situations I could normally [deal with]. I was running on past empty and the smallest thing [made me] fall to pieces. Those close to me described [me] as being negative, introverted and very unwell. I was often tearful and lacked physical strength. Recovery was gradual over the next fifteen years.

Reflecting on it now, I think it is very important to look at your lifestyle and make changes where needed. You have to think about your body, first and foremost, as everything else stems from it. I saw a nutritionist and took some food supplements. I worked on my physical fitness and began to treat my body with respect and love. I didn't drive myself so much. I began to listen to my body, to recognize warning signs, such as being very tired or tearful. I made adjustments to my commitments and expectations of myself; I found that I needed to say no at times. I learned to see relaxing and recharging myself as important. We all make mistakes and we need to be kind to ourselves when things go wrong and learn not to take ourselves so seriously. When you are at the bottom of the pit hope seems nowhere to be found. Yet there is hope. You can't press eject and get out of it. It's a walking through.

This chapter focuses on what we can do to improve our physical and emotional well-being as we recover from burnout. It connects with what we said about creating a sense of personal space and a good routine in Chapter 7.

Since suffering from burnout you may have neglected exercise, or not been able to do it. Your diet may have become unhealthy. We are so busy coping with the demands and pressures on us that we forget how to listen to our physical bodies, or misunderstand what they are telling us. Consequently we become completely depleted and exhausted and burnt out.

Margaret's recovery involved her trying to regain healthy habits of diet and exercise and relaxation, and we will now look at these. You should visit your doctor if you feel unwell, and take any advice or medication you may need. Beth, as we have seen, became physically ill and needed time off work and medication. On returning to work, Beth reduced her hours to enable her to have time to look after herself while her son was at school. She realized work was no longer her priority any more. Even though she took these precautions she became ill again a year later, requiring light therapy for her severe rash.

If your mental health is poor, you should seek help with that too.

Diet

From our food we draw nutrients to revitalize and replenish our diminished resources and to manufacture the chemicals and building blocks our bodies need, so it is important to make sure we have a sensible and varied diet. Our bodies need regular, healthy and varied meals of wholesome food. A recent survey showed that millions of young professionals only cook once a week and live on quick-fix meals. Eight out of ten said that they would cook more often if they arrived home from work at a decent time.[1]

When we are under pressure, we may only have time to eat junk food, or find ourselves dependent on large amounts of caffeine or nicotine to get us going in the morning and large volumes of alcohol to relax us in the evenings, with the result that our sense of taste becomes reduced. Adjusting to moderate consumption can prove difficult and we may need help and advice about healthy eating, and so rediscover our taste. We can combine this with taking up an interest in cooking and preparing meals, as John did.

There are numerous books, blogs and websites about different diets, and resources giving guidance on ideal body weight for our height and age. Some are mentioned in the Resources section. If you prefer talking to someone, speak to a nurse or nutritionist at your GP's surgery.

Fitness and exercise

It is a good idea to have a medical check-up and blood tests before you start exercising in order to get fit, particularly if you have got out of condition. It is always advisable to start with gentle exercise and then build up to more strenuous exercise. No one form is better than another, but you need to set attainable goals to maintain your motivation. Exercising with others can be helpful, as you won't be tempted to drop out so easily if it involves letting someone else down. Be realistic about how much you can do, perhaps starting off with five minutes of gentle exercise each day and gradually increasing the time spent and how hard it is.

When we exercise, our body temperature rises slightly and this can help ease muscle tension, much like using a hot tub, jacuzzi or sauna. Exercising also takes our mind off work and worries, and makes us feel good about ourselves. Whatever we choose to do, it should be something we enjoy, or we will soon stop doing it. Here are a few ideas:

- walking

- jogging

- gardening

- vacuuming or other housework

- team sports

- swimming

- dancing

- going to the gym

- Pilates

- yoga.

Find something that appeals to you – perhaps something you used to do, or try something totally new. The most important thing is to do some regular exercise. John had been very athletic and sporty in his youth, but as life got busier he had cut out playing a lot of sport. On the advice of his stress counsellor he joined a volleyball team and played each week. He says he enjoyed the camaraderie and feeling more relaxed after the game.

A good further guide to the medical benefits of exercise and some do's and don'ts are found in chapter 15 of James Scala's *25 Natural Ways to Manage Stress and Avoid Burnout.*

Nature

If we exercise outdoors we can enjoy the fresh air, and it can be very restorative to be in touch with natural things. Various rehabilitative centres for people recovering from addictions use working with the land or with animals as a means of recuperation and readjustment. People's lives have become more urban, and long days are spent working indoors in cities or towns, meaning we rarely see or notice anything natural. So whether we take indoor or outdoor exercise, it can be extremely helpful to take an interest in nature. Here are some suggestions:

- keeping animals (anything from stick insects to sheep!)

- having a bird table

- going for walks

- visiting wildlife centres

- growing indoor plants

- tending a garden

- visiting a city farm

- taking up horse riding.

Fun and play

Into this mix we need to add some fun and playfulness. Laughter and play increase the efficiency of our immune system and our physical well-being. This helps us recoup our energy levels and reduces stress, which is vital if we are going to live in a more balanced way.

We need to rediscover ways to relax and unwind. We have mentioned simple relaxation techniques in Chapter 7 on creating space. Here we are thinking about having fun. Prior to becoming burnt out, you will have been driven and focused, and have probably lost the childhood skill of drifting through a day, being flexible and receptive to what is around. Even if you have managed to continue playing sport, you may have pushed and driven yourself in that area too, seeking to excel. So relearning the art of play and enjoyment for its own sake is vital. It is important to nurture and develop the child within us throughout our lives, that inner person who can be delighted and surprised.

Think over when and how and if you play. It might be a sport or an outdoor pursuit of some other kind. Or it could be as simple as playing board games, cards or Wii with children or grandchildren, doing a jigsaw, or simply allowing yourself time to drift and be playful without having an agenda. Pick up an old hobby, or try something new. One of the hallmarks of a playful activity is that it will be absorbing and you will enjoy it. Whatever you do, give it regular space and time. Playing will help your recovery.

Sex

Finally in this chapter we need to think a bit about our sexual life. Under the strain of stress and burnout we may find our sex drive markedly reduced, or channelled into unhealthy things such as Internet pornography, as we lack energy or time to pursue normal relationships. If we need to take medication, side effects can adversely affect our sex lives, and we should talk to our doctor about them, even if it feels embarrassing. It is important to address this to enable us to have a healthy sex life in the future. For other advice or help in this area, there are sex therapists or sexual health clinics advertising in the Yellow Pages or online. Bona fide therapists are registered with the British Association of Counsellors and Psychotherapists, so check this, as many unqualified people advertise services. Hopefully with more time and space, a more balanced lifestyle, and other creative activities, the libido will return to normal.

13

How Can I Recover
My Creativity?

Interview: Austin

Austin is a thirty-six-year-old art director who is still recovering from burnout. Working in a creative field didn't protect him from burnout when his workload increased. Austin says:

I moved to a new job, and initially all was well as I instigated new work projects… My wife and I were living in a rundown home [which needed] refurbishment, doing the building work ourselves. Suddenly my workload dramatically increased… work took over my life. I was working on the train and arrived early… I worked through my lunch hour and at home. Despite raising my concerns with my bosses, they did not do anything. The following month several team members went on holiday, coinciding with the end of my probationary period. The added pressure tipped me over the edge. Physically I felt very tired all the time but couldn't sleep. My mind and my heart were racing. I often felt sick or vomited before going to work, and lost my appetite. I became grumpy, touchy and impatient, with mood swings. I began to worry about the future and how to pay the bills. Spiritually I felt dry, and lost my sense of connectedness. Others found me distracted and forgetful, not my usual happy self. I couldn't remember appointments or plans I had made.

I went to see my GP (and had a minor car accident on the way) and was signed off work.

My family offered me emotional and practical support, and my workplace offered me all the time I needed on statutory sick pay. I found myself sitting at home wallowing in self-pity and feeling sick. I decided to quit my job and to do some freelance work [but it] didn't bear fruit financially. My wife had a stressful job move and we slowly ran out of money. My wife became very unwell and this piled on pressure for me to get better. Then my nan became ill and died. I became increasingly depressed and anxious and took on a job I didn't enjoy simply to pay the bills.

My confidence in my professional ability and at home has taken a severe beating. I am having regular counselling. I am seeking to change my lifestyle. I am drinking less caffeine and taking regular exercise which makes me feel better. I am eating regular meals and getting up by 8 a.m. each day. I am seeking to think more positively. I'm making sure I do things. Rather than watch TV in [the] evening I try to do an odd job on the house so several are not waiting for me at the weekend. I feel progress is being made, but all my energy is placed in getting through today and I can't plan for the future yet.

....

Everybody is gifted in many ways. The workplace rarely uses all of our natural gifts, nor does it often allow time for our other abilities and creative instincts to develop. This is in a normal working situation. In burnout, we have not usually been drawing on the majority of our creative talents. Most of them will have lain dormant while one of two of them may have been overused.

Even when we have had the opportunity for leisure it has probably had to be used for zoning out, sleeping, doing housework, or childcare. There will have been little time for properly taking leisure – or recreation, as it might be better termed. The word "recreation" can be split into re-creation and this is what good use of leisure time should be doing for us: re-creating our inner selves, rebuilding our resources. Nor should this simply be seen as a chance to recharge our batteries, as it is often expressed, as if we were a working machine. This implies all our real significance is in our work. This is not a healthy view of life. A healthy person has an array of ways of expressing their inner creativity.

EXPLORING CREATIVITY

This chapter concentrates on our creative giftings, and rediscovering and re-energizing those that have lain untouched. Doing so will make us more whole, healthier people, and may lead on to us seeking a new path in life in the future. Exploring our other talents could open up a new direction for our future employment. The more our regular employment uses our natural giftings, the happier we will be and the better we will fulfil the demands of that employment. Other people around us will benefit too: a deeper benefit to exploring our creative selves. It may prove to be a voyage of discovery. We may well find out new things about ourselves, hidden talents which we didn't know were there. This can be fun.

Finally, exploring our creative side can give voice to deep things within us that defy expression. Being creative accords with our souls at a deep level. We know not how or why. We just know that it is immensely significant to us.

So here are a number of exercises to try in order to revivify your creative side.

Exercise 1
Write down any recreational things that you have longed to do more of but have had to shelve because of work commitments.

Exercise 2

Read through the list of recreational activities given below, and score each one from 0 to 5, where 0 is "Not interested at all" and 5 is "I would have a strong interest in this". Don't worry about whether you think you would be competent at this activity – the point is to gauge interest and enthusiasm. Possible recreational activities include:

- painting and fine arts
- craftwork
- sewing
- tapestry
- sculpture
- pottery
- textile work
- music
- acting
- watching theatre
- literature
- writing
- gardening
- climbing
- fell walking
- running
- cycling
- DIY
- swimming
- organized team sports
- sailing
- dancing
- horse riding
- archery.

Add to the list anything you have done in the past which you had to give up because of work pressure. But be prepared to consider new things, where you may discover new talents. See if they touch an urge within you.

Exercise 3
Pick out your three highest scores from the list above, and write a paragraph on each activity, answering the following questions in each case:

- I scored this activity higher than the others because…

- I would like to get into this activity because…

- If I found I could do this activity, I would feel…

- If somebody asked me why I did this activity, I would say to them…

Plainly, these statements overlap, but we give the four of them to help push your thoughts when answering, exploring the possibilities as fully as you can. The important thing is to imagine yourself doing these activities. Don't worry that you may not be any good at them, or that pursuing them might mean attending a class as a beginner. Just let your imagination and enthusiasm roam freely.

Exercise 4
After a day or two, look at the list again. Do you think the same way? Would you give the activities the same score? Are there any others to add?

Exercise 5
Decide which three activities you would like to major on, or whether you are going to try to do them all.

Exercise 6
Make a plan. What are you going to do in order to be able to pursue this activity? Do you need to join a club, take lessons, buy certain equipment, work out how you are going to find the

time and the money? Do you need to discuss it with anyone else? Where should you start?

Exercise 7

Put the things you need to do in order, deciding what the first move is, then the second, and when you are going to do them. Commit this to paper. Incidentally, would it help to have a buddy or a coach alongside you?

Examples

- Heather found walking and going to rugby matches therapeutic.

- John was encouraged to buy a season ticket to attend rugby matches at weekends. He found shouting for his team each week very cathartic, as a means to reduce stress.

- Michael rediscovered the enjoyment of reading for pleasure, going to the cinema, and setting a regular time to see good friends once a month with his wife.

- Lily found that getting back to her former recreation of knitting was an important part of her recovery from burnout. She had been able to devote more time to craftwork previously but had stopped because of time needed to care for her mother and the house. Getting back to it was part of her way of regaining some time to herself, boosting her self-worth and feeling she could have some life of her own.

FINALLY

Hopefully these exercises are enough to get you started out on this vital journey to re-creation.

A final warning: we need to be aware that we often shrink back from being creative. There is a terrible inclination in human nature to emphasize the negative and bury the positive, shunning and avoiding it. Creativity is deeply positive and right. We can be almost frightened of our creativity. When we have done some creative work, such as writing a short story, highly destructive self-critical feelings usually pour in from somewhere. Julia Cameron, whose internationally best-selling book *The Artist's Way* encourages people to rediscover their innate creativity, calls this "The savage inner critic". She has a special chapter on overwork, or workaholism as she calls it, and the creative. In it she says:

> *Workaholism is an addiction and like all addictions it blocks creative energy… Play can make the workaholic nervous, fun is scary… In order to recover our creativity we must learn to see workaholism as a block instead of a building block. Work abuse creates in our artist a Cinderella Complex. We are always dreaming of the ball and always experiencing the ball and chain.*[1]

We can rob ourselves of important freedoms very easily. If you have fears, decide to ignore them and give something a go. Don't let the truly creative be a no-go area.

14

How Can I Have a Wider Outlook on Life?

Burnout will have narrowed our view of life. We end up concentrating on the job in hand, and our entire attention is funnelled exclusively into work. Among the many damaging aspects of this is the loss of a broader view of life. Most work is very specialized. If we become completely absorbed in it then we will lose a sense of what is going on in the world at large, not giving real thought to bigger values than just getting the job done.

As we have so often said in this book, we believe burnout can be turned from a disaster into an opportunity. It offers a chance to recoup important ground and a wider worldview, perhaps for the first time since we entered our adult life. There are many other areas of wider cultural life that could be worth exploring, and we consider some of them here. As with the previous chapter on creativity, no one will be able to pursue all these areas, but they may lead to new involvements and even new careers.

POLITICS

We may already have clear political alignments, although the majority of us do not. The national trend is away from membership of political parties towards a more free-floating approach. If you have never been involved much in politics, try dipping a toe in the water.

- Attend your national congress or parliament for some of the debates.

- Sit in the public gallery of local authority council meetings, completely free of charge.

- Visit your MP at one of their surgeries. They will gladly give time to talk about why they have become an MP and why they are interested in politics, even if you have no particular issues to raise. They will be pleasantly surprised to receive such an enquiry instead of another set of complaints.

- At election time, read the parties' manifestos. Decide if you align with any of the political parties sufficiently to join them and become an activist.

- Try drafting an opinion article such as the ones in all the daily newspapers. See how yours compares and what your friends make of it.

- Follow political blogs and tweets of every shade of opinion, and then try making your own comments or at least drafting them and showing them to people to see if they would stand up in the public sphere.

- Become involved in some public issue that engages your concerns, whether local, national or international.

- Support movements, such as Amnesty International, that defend victims of conscience, by taking their literature and maybe donating to them.

TRAVEL

Travelling is excellent for broadening the mind and refreshing our outlook on life's possibilities. Just getting away can have great benefit in itself, wherever we go, but absorbing a different place and way of being can add an extra dimension of discovering meaning. I (Andrew) had six weeks off after becoming suicidal, spent walking the Northern Fells. I didn't do anything especially cultural other than the walking, but I came home able to work again and have never been burnt out since. I recall one night as I lay my head on the pillow at the B&B having a wonderful moment when the whole panoply of the day's walking played before my mind's eye like a symphony. I realized then that long distance walking was for me a profound resource. I have tried to do some every year since.

After having to stop work, Ed booked himself in for two weeks' mountain climbing and glacier walking in Switzerland. He recalls walking all day long in a whiteout. He was safe, linked to the others by ropes, but otherwise lost in solitude amid a world of snow, with no other visibility. He found this strongly restorative. It has stayed with him ever since as a formative experience. Justin found that his new job with a charity gave him plenty of opportunities to travel, which he enjoyed.

Here are a few obvious steps to help you get away travelling.

- Think about where you would like to go. In burnout, we often shy away from the positive, but we need to allow our imagination free rein. Try getting out an atlas and seeing what parts of the world attract you, or watch travel programmes and imagine yourself in these places. Give yourself permission to imagine possibilities, overcoming any negative voices saying you shouldn't be thinking this way.

- Decide how you want to reach your destination. This too should be pleasurable. Anticipating the boat trip or train journey or whatever is fun – and part of recovery. These days we can surf the net for all manner of travel deals. There may be alternative ways to travel which would add to the benefit of it.

- Consider how active you want your time away to be. For some of us, a relaxing holiday with little activity will be the best. For others, something more demanding – whether physically, mentally, or both – will be better.

- Do you want to go alone or with others? This will depend on practical considerations of cost and availability, no doubt. But it is important to think through which is best for you, as a person recovering from burnout. Do you thrive more in solitude than in company? Even if you have a clear preference about this, as perhaps discovered doing the Myers-Briggs personality indicator, maybe you will gain more re-creation by doing something different on the journey from your normal preference.

- Consider what kind of accommodation you want. Here too there will be questions of expense, but what would be the most refreshing? What would provide the best cultural change?

It is good to keep a blog or a journal of any travelling. Consider taking some time each day to write down your reflections, and include photographs and film. This cements the value of what you are learning and keeps it in permanent form for later reference. It is surprising how much and how quickly we forget.

CULTURE

Entering into the world of culture broadens us as people – whether that is our own culture or another one. Consider exploring some of the following areas in your own culture:

- art
- architecture
- music
- theatre
- philosophy
- history
- literature.

Ways of engaging could include:

- enrolling in an evening class
- signing up for a formal learning course, if you want something more rigorous
- using a local resource, such as the local library
- getting a good book on your chosen subject
- visiting galleries
- taking a city break in the UK to study its architecture
- going to performances, plays, concerts
- joining or starting up a local book/play reading group or a music appreciation group
- signing up to conducted tours of significant buildings
- starting to write an historical novel or short story.

Go with your initial enthusiasm, making a start where you think you would most enjoy it.

Other cultures

It is also good to look in depth at another culture, different from your own. The resources for this have never been better with the availability of the Internet, and also with a greater internationalism prevailing. Bruce and Katherine Epperly in their book on burnout, *Feed the Fire*, stress the value of engaging with other cultures to combat burnout.[1] Here are a few options:

- Chinese

- Japanese

- Indian

- Polynesian

- African

- Asiatic

- Middle Eastern

- Australian.

We might engage in building awareness of another culture in one of the following ways:

- language studies, perhaps left over from school or even university, which have had to be shelved because of work pressure

- travel, as we have just mentioned above

- cuisine – it's fun to try different ways to eat and cook foods from other cultures

- festivals – go along and sample the atmosphere

- befriending – most of us will already have friends or colleagues from other cultures. If we don't, it's not too difficult to meet such people. Conversations in which we ask to be told about how these friends feel about the ordinary things in life – births, marriages, funerals etc. – can be useful windows into another culture.

If we can't get out to do these things, we could do them at home, using the Internet or books. If we are completely broke financially, a lot of good material is available free of charge through the library service, which provides books, films and many other resources. We might prefer to take a particular theme such as film or photography or wildlife and look at that in different parts of the world, and write on it. All of this may seem miles away from our problems of employment, weariness and so on but if we are able to do any of it, it is very relevant indeed. It is refreshing and replenishes our inner soul, restoring a right balance and humanity to us. In time it will benefit those around us because we will be more interesting and more complete for doing it, and then it may help us in planning a healthier future.

PHILANTHROPY

It is another good thing when we are in burnout to think about supporting a good cause and giving something of ourselves, expecting no reward. This may seem odd when we are ourselves in need of support but, once we have recovered sufficiently from the early times of total exhaustion, helping others can be healing for us as well as good for them. It gives a due sense of doing something truly worthwhile, some lasting good, however little. This can be curative where a component in our burnout has been despair that all our hard work has not actually amounted to anything significant.

If our burnout has included an element of over-caring for those in need, as is commonly the case, we will need to show some caution here. It might be that if this is so we are wiser to leave philanthropy alone until we are clearer about the necessary boundaries between ourselves and the needy. Nonetheless, some philanthropy is a hallmark of a healthy emotional and moral life and it is good to consider involving ourselves in it when we can.

There are boundless charities and good causes both in our own country and abroad. You probably already have at least a passing interest in certain charities. If your circumstances mean that you have now got more time than before, there are huge opportunities to give of your time and energy into charitable work, and also to raise funds for charity in quite enjoyable ways, by cycling or other sponsored events of all kinds. You will probably find that you enjoy it, learn a lot and meet a whole variety of new people that you would not have met otherwise.

These are just some ways to overcome the narrowing effect of burnout. They can interconnect and be adapted. They also interconnect with topics in the other chapters in this section. No matter. Feel free to dip in and mix as it seems best to you.

15

How Do I Face the Future?

. . . .

This is the final chapter of the book, reviewing your overall situation. How can you face the future and ensure that burnout does not recur? There are a series of steps that you can take, drawing on the material in your journal, the decisions you have made, and the things you have realized about yourself.

IS MY JOB RIGHT FOR ME?

One huge question that needs answering is: "Is my job – or whatever commitments brought me to burnout – right for me?" A career change may not be possible, but thinking about it can be productive. Any full-time job we do inevitably takes the lion's share of our time. So finding the full-time occupation that suits us best is vital, to be engaged most deeply and be most inspired. Being in the wrong job, or a job that has become the wrong job, is misery. So we need to look back and work out why we are where we are in our employment history and ask: "What took me into my previous/existing job?"

Thinking about what took you into your most recent job:

- Was it your choice, or only partly?

- If only partly, who else was involved, and to what extent?

- Was it dictated by circumstances?

- What factors influenced you?

It is worth writing this down in your journal. It is surprising that people often enter careers almost by default early in life. I (Andrew) nearly became a lawyer and very nearly trained in central London, just because of a casual recommendation by a careers master when I was fifteen. In fact, both things would have been disastrous for me. I much prefer being out of the city and in a less structured workplace.

Sometimes people have chosen a degree at university when quite young and immature, not knowing much about the world or about themselves. Once they have a degree, they take employment in the field that they are qualified for, and can find themselves in a career that is not fully their own choice. So we should take some time to go back over those early days when we first chose our career and see how much it was in fact our own choice.

In so far as it was the choice of others, write down the answers to the following:

- Who were they?

- How much did you respect them?

- Why was their advice so influential?

- What would you do now if they were giving you the same advice?

- How would you respond?

In so far as it was your own choice, review that choice now with the experience of the years and self-understanding, writing the answers to the questions below in your journal.

- What would you say to the young you and to others as you entered that area of work?

- What hopes and motivations were in play?

- What feelings did that young person have?

- Were those feelings idealistic or mercenary?

- Were they feelings of excitement or resignation?

- Were they feelings of ambition, or happiness to retain a lowly status?

- Was there a strong theoretical philosophy or was the aim more practical?

- Do I still have the same hopes, feelings and emotions as I had then, or have they changed over the years?

- Note down what has changed and in what way.

GLEANING THE GOOD

Even if we have reached the point where we think the whole time we spent working was a complete waste of our life and talents, it may be possible to glean something good from it.

Here are some suggestions to try to glean the good from the past.

- List all the people at work you have met and admired.

- Write their names down and write a sentence or two about each.

- What was it about them that you liked?

- What debt do you feel you owe to them?

- Are you still in touch with them? If not, is it practicable to get back in touch?

- Make a list of people you did not like. Did they have any saving graces at all? They are unlikely to have been without any redeeming features, even though it may have seemed that way by the time things got difficult. It is important for your own sake to try to keep a sense of perspective. What do you think motivated them, even if you did not like their behaviour?

- What lessons for the good do you feel you have learned? Maybe write down something along the lines of "My time at that employment taught me this". Even if this is quite a bitter lesson, at least you have learned it.

WHAT NEEDS TO CHANGE?

If you were to go back into your old job situation, what would have to change about it for you to be able to feel motivated and productive in it? This might be its overall size, its geographical location, its work ethic, its management structures, its philosophy, the pay and the staffing levels – anything.

If those things could change, would going back to your old job be a realistic proposition? Could you have a fruitful second phase of a career? What would need to happen for this to be so?

If you do feel there might be a way into some branch of your chosen career, how will you avoid getting burnt out again? If you can settle that in your mind, then maybe you can look around for openings in your profession with these criteria, perhaps by using a specialist employment agency, or by studying the vacancies.

DREAM THE DREAM

We may feel we have no choice about changing what we do, that we are only qualified in one field and we need to earn money and support dependants. Put that aside for a moment; imagine all things are possible and think of a change of work as being something that can be achieved. Forget all practical barriers, financial considerations, and those of space, time, family and so on. If you had a complete choice of field of employment, what would you do? Dream the dream! Allow the initial vague ideas to take some form and write them down. They may be in complete conflict with each other and not sound at all practical, but that does not matter as long as they appeal to you.

- Where would you be?

- What would you be doing?

- Who would be with you?

- What sort of house would you have?

- What sort of clothing would you be wearing?

- Why is it so appealing?

- What is it that makes you dream about it in this way and makes you want to do it?

Put your list away for quite a while, at least a week, and then return to it and see how much of it sticks, and how much begins to seem like a fairy tale. Work with the persistent bits and see if they hammer out into something firmer. Beware, you can be so embarrassed by your deepest wishes that you regard them as silly and throw them away. But they can be linked to your deepest self and be the clue to a really happy life – so go carefully.

Reality test
Once you have worked out the main themes of your dream future, then comes the time to give them a reality test. Can it really be done? How would it feel if you did make that move and, once the shine had worn off, been there a year? Two years? Three years? How would it affect your deepest relationships – your spouse or partner, your children, your friendships? Is it compatible with keeping them? There are money issues always – can you afford it?

Once you do come to a conclusion about pursuing your dream, you will need to check your emotions. If you feel excited, and can't stop thinking about the new direction, or even dreaming about it, these are good indicators. But if you have decided to put it aside, are you feeling relieved or do you think you may have buried something important? Have you a sense of deep disappointment in deciding not to go ahead?

So far, all these exercises can be done on your own. But it is really helpful, of course, in planning a new future, to involve an array of other people before taking major life-changing steps, such as your partner and friends, therapists or mentors.

Ed shared his plans with those around him and changed direction for the better. Through the support of his wife and close friends, he began to look at the alternative career options available and set about planning a new start that would combine work and home life in a more balanced way. Ed says, "Ask yourself if you have a supportive network around you and whether you have empowered them to give you honest feedback. If you have, are you receptive to it? And try to get feedback from as many sources as are relevant."

EDUCATING NEAREST AND DEAREST ABOUT BURNOUT

Research has shown that people close to a person experiencing burnout have frequently lacked knowledge about burnout and its challenges, and sometimes feel that they are putting their own lives on hold to help.[1] Anything that you have found useful in deepening your understanding about what has happened to you in burnout, and how to deal with it, would also be valuable resources for those close to you. It will help them to more fully appreciate what you have gone/are going through, as well as giving them ideas about what they might helpfully do to be supportive to you. It will help them to understand that recovery takes time, and to be realistic and perhaps reduce their frustration with you when things do not progress as quickly as they hope. You may want to share any books or information you have found helpful, and encourage them to read them and talk about burnout with you.

WHAT NEXT?

Before we embark on a new venture, or indeed pick up from where we left off, we should review what we have learned during our experience of burnout. We have looked at what caused us to burn out in the first place, and begun to understand ourselves better than before. We have given ourselves permission to stop doing certain things that contributed to our getting burnout, and have had some space and time to develop a better work/life balance. We have reflected on and put into practice a variety of lifestyle changes that will be protective to us and enable us to take downtime and recover between bouts of stress. We have a sharper and clearer idea of what our personal values are.

Making resolutions

Now is a good time to go back over any notes you made in your journal, to refresh your memory and decide some clear resolutions and intentions for the future. You might want to take up a new sport or pastime. In your journal you can record your plan of action to make this happen. You may have big hopes, such as your dream job, or small ideas, such as planting seeds. For some of us it is helpful if we record our immediate plans – some we hope and intend to have in place in the next six months, and some in the next five years.

It might be a good idea to note in your diary the important times of rest and recovery well ahead, before other commitments crowd in, and keep them as sacrosanct.

You might want to commit to paper what you have resolved.

Here are a few suggestions, but add your own:

- I will not try to be all things to all people.

- I will not spread myself too thinly.

- I will sometimes leave things unfinished.

- I will learn to say no.

- I will schedule time for myself and those around me.

- I will switch off and do nothing regularly.

- I will stop being my own worst enemy and seek to become my own best friend.

Good ideas for how to make them stick are to

- write them out

- pin them up where you will look at them regularly

- carry them in your wallet or purse

- reread them frequently until they become a deep part of you, because unless your inner attitudes shift, your good intentions will remain only that – intentions

- share them with a buddy and meet up regularly to monitor how you are doing

- condense them into a motto to live by.

Everything that we have looked at is designed to help us live satisfying, productive and joyful lives. The experience of burnout, or getting close to it, gives us a golden opportunity to become more fully human and alive.

Interview: Michael

We want to end this book by leaving you with Michael's story. Michael is a thirty-three-year-old church leader and minister.

When I was thirty I had been in charge of my church for five years. I knew I had been living on empty for a long time as there had been constant demands on my physical, emotional and spiritual energies. I felt I had been giving out repeatedly. I realized I was unwell.

There was a definite, noticeable "moment" when it felt like something inside had broken. There was a very clear "before" and "after". I was in a leadership meeting where a normally routine example of robust discussion and opposition seemed to floor me. I had never experienced anything like the sensation before, and I knew then that something serious was going on. I tried carrying on... until I was leading a church meeting about three days later, with a room full of 100 people, when all I can say is that it felt like I was having an out-of-body experience. It was like I was a robot, just going through the motions, watching myself lead the meeting but I wasn't really present in the room. I have very few memories of that meeting, and I couldn't concentrate at all during [it]. It was the next day that I went to the doctor, and he signed me off for six weeks. I found I couldn't concentrate on anything for a couple of weeks.

On reflection, I... remember over the months before that I had struggled to find any joy [while] spending time with my young children, which now I realize was... a strong indication something was wrong. After the "moment" when it felt like something inside had broken, there were many symptoms. After seeing the doctor, it was the first time I had wept in a long, long time. I couldn't walk into public spaces, I was fearful of entering Tesco's or seeing anyone.

I had no real understanding from work and little support was offered to my wife, who had to cope with me not being able to do much. My wife and close family were very supportive and thoughtful. Also, close friends wrote and texted. One invited me to a football [match] when I had been off work for a month, and that meant a great deal to me.

Two things in particular helped me get better. One was buying a journal to record and process my journey. My journal became like a friend to me during those weeks and months… In those early weeks when I couldn't speak very much I felt it was easier to write my questions, hurts and prayers.

The second was going on a led retreat. I was alone, but there was community there that was very loving, giving me the space that I needed but offering prayer when I wanted it. The person leading reflections for the week had a good combination of humour and honesty. He was like a gift. I was able to laugh and cry during sessions. The retreat kick-started exercise such as walking, which became a pattern of my time off.

When I got home I did anything that was "tank-filling", things that re-created me.

I now worry less about the small things. I no longer think that I have to be superhuman. I value my family much more, and think of my work in ministry differently.

I am now more alert to signs that emotional exhaustion is coming on. Although I have very busy weeks and months without a lot of thought for energy levels, I take evasive action much more often, without apology, to spend time doing re-creative things like walking, reading for pleasure, the cinema, and setting a regular time to see good friends once a month with my wife.

I didn't really see anyone [while] I recovered, but once I had had six weeks off work, I felt more human and alive than I had done in years.

. . . .

We hope that you will be able to echo Michael's final words, *"I felt more human and alive than I had done in years."* We have repeated throughout our book that we believe burnout can be a great opportunity to recover our humanity, indeed to discover it for the first time in many ways. We hope you come to a place of full recovery and good health.

Resources

. . . .

GENERAL BOOKS ON BURNOUT

Donna Andronicos, *Coping with Burnout,* London: SPCK, 2009.

Cary Cherniss, *Beyond Burnout: Helping Teachers, Nurses, Therapists and Lawyers Recover From Stress and Disillusionment,* London: Routledge, 1995.

Todd Duncan, *Life on the Wire,* Nashville, TN: Thomas Nelson, 2010.

Dina Glouberman, *The Joy of Burnout,* London: Hodder & Stoughton, 2002.

Bruce and Katherine Epperly, *Feed the Fire,* Cleveland, OH: Pilgrim Press, 2008.

Ivan Herald, *Don't Just Do Something, Sit There!* Baulkham Hills, NSW: Oz Fame, 1997.

Kate Middleton, *Stress: How to De-stress Without Doing Less,* Oxford: Lion Books, 2009.

Ken Powell, *Burnout: What Happens When Stress Gets Out of Control,* London: Thorsons, 1993.

STRESS TESTS

http://www.mindtools.com – go to stress management to access the Holmes and Rahe Stress Scale

http://www.thecounselingteam.com/interactive/

www.isma.org.uk

BURNOUT MEASURES

http://www.mindtools.com/stress/Brn/BurnoutSelfTest.htm
http://www.worktolive.info/burnout-prevention/
http://www.mnsu.edu/hr/profdev/handouts/handouts05/
  burnout.pdf

SUICIDAL FEELINGS

The Samaritans, Freepost RSRB-KKBY-CYJK, Chris, PO Box 9090, Stirling, FK8 2SA. Tel. 08457 90 90 90. www.samaritans.org

RELAXATION EXERCISES

www.netdoctor.co.uk
www.thistimethisspace.com

MEDITATION TECHNIQUES

www.freemindfulness.org
Matthew Johnstone, *Quiet the Mind: An Illustrated Guide on How to Meditate,* London: Constable & Robinson, 2012.

RELATIONSHIPS

The Forgiveness Project, www.theforgivenessproject.com

COUNSELLING

British Association of Counselling and Psychotherapy, BACP House, 15 St John's Business Park, Lutterworth, LE17 4HB. Tel: 01455 883300, www.bacp.co.uk
American Psychological Association: www.apa.org
American Psychotherapy Association:
  www.americanpsychotherapy.com
Australian and New Zealand Association of Psychotherapy Ltd (ANZAP): www.anzapweb.com

Psychotherapy & Counselling Federation of Australia (PACFA):
   www.pacfa.org.au
New Zealand Association of Psychotherapists (NZAP):
   www.nzap.org.NZ

COGNITIVE BEHAVIOURAL THERAPY

www.moodgym.org
www.llttf.com
www.beatingtheblues.co.uk
All three of these are free online CBT self-help websites.
www.rscpp.co.uk for telephone counselling.

PERSONALITY INDICATORS

www.myersbriggs.org
www.humanmetrics.com
ocean.visualdna.com
personalitydesk.com
discover-your-type.com

LIFE COACHING

International Association of Life Coaches:
   www.iaplifecoaches.org
Life Coaching in the UK: www.lifecoach-directory.org.uk
Life Coaching Institute of Australia: www.lcia.com.au
Australian Life Coaching Society: www.lifecoaching.net.au
Life Coaching Institute of America:
   www.lifecoachingamerica.com

PROFESSIONAL MENTORING

Spirit Business Enterprises, Cygnet House, 12–14 Sydenham
   Road, Croydon, Surrey CR0 2EE. Tel. 07538 091 974.
   www.spiritbusinessenterprises.co.uk
www.careerscast.com

RETREATS

www.retreats.org.uk (Christian)
www.goingonretreat.com (Buddhist)
www.mindfulnessretreats.co.uk for stress reduction

YOGA

www.nhs.uk – enter yoga as a search term on the site

HEALTH AND FITNESS

Diet/BMI: nhibisupport.com/bmi gives advice about healthy
    eating too.
James Scala, *25 Natural Ways to Manage Stress and Avoid
    Burnout*, New Canaan, CT: Keats Publishing, 2000, gives
    lots of practical advice in this area.

CREATIVITY

Julia Cameron, *The Artist's Way: A Course in Discovering and
    Recovering Your Creative Self,* London: Pan Books, 1993. An
    international best-seller and a good place to start.

End Notes

· · · · · · · · · · · · · ·

PART ONE

Chapter 1

1. Ulrich Kraft, quoting H. Freudenberger and G. North in "Burned Out", *Scientific American Mind*, June/July 2006, pp. 28–33.

2. Glenn Roberts, "Prevention of Burnout", *Advances in Psychiatric Treatment*, Vol. 3, 1997, p. 283.

3. Glenn Roberts, "Prevention of Burnout", p. 283

4. Dina Glouberman, *The Joy of Burnout*, London: Hodder & Stoughton, 2002, p. 60.

5. Glenn Roberts, "Prevention of Burnout", p. 284.

6. Jonny Wilkinson, *Jonny: My Autobiography*, London: Headline Publishing, 2011, quoted in *The Times*, 8 November 2011.

7. Geraint Anderson, *Cityboy*, London: Headline Publishing, 2009, quoted in *The Times*, 8 November 2011.

8. Jonny Wilkinson, *Jonny: My Autobiography*.

9. Jonny Wilkinson, *Jonny: My Autobiography*.

Chapter 2

1. Kate Middleton, *Stress: How to De-stress Without Doing Less*, Oxford: Lion Books, 2009, p. 13.

Chapter 3

1. R.M. Yerkes and J.D. Dobson, "The Relation of Strength of Stimulus to Rapidity of Habit Formation", *Journal of*

Comparative Neurology and Psychology 18, 1908, pp. 459–482.
2. Bette Midler interview in *The Times, times2*, 18 December 2012.
3. The Chartered Institute of Personnel and Development, "Work-related stress: What the law says", September 2010, p. 5, found on cipd.co.uk (accessed 19 June 2013).
4. Thomas Holmes and Richard Rahe, "The Social Readjustment Rating Scale", *Journal of Psychosomatic Research*, Vol. 1, Issue 2, pp. 213–18.

Chapter 4
1. Donna Andronicos, *Coping with Burnout*, London: SPCK, 2009, p. 7.
2. James Scala, *25 Natural Ways to Manage Stress and Avoid Burnout*, New Canaan, CT: Keats Publishing, 2000, p. 30.
3. Ken Powell, *Burnout*, London: Thorsons, 1993, p. 67.
4. Cary Cherniss, *Beyond Burnout: Helping Teachers, Nurses, Therapists and Lawyers Recover From Stress and Disillusionment*, London: Routledge, 1995, p. 32.

Chapter 5
1. Ken Powell, *Burnout*, p. 63.
2. S. Sonnetag, C. Binnewies, E.J. Mojza, "Staying well and engaged when demands are high: the role of psychological detachment", *Journal of Applied Psychology* 95(5), 2010, pp. 965–976.
3. Dina Glouberman, *The Joy of Burnout*, p. 29.
4. The Chartered Institute of Personnel and Development, "Work-related stress: What the law says", September 2010, p. 9, found on cipd.co.uk (accessed 19 June 2013).
5. Glenn Roberts, "Prevention of Burnout", p. 283.

PART TWO

Chapter 7

1. B. Gaede, "Burnout – a personal journey", *South African Family Practice* 47 (4), 2005, pp. 5–6.

2. Dina Glouberman, *The Joy of Burnout*, pp. 115, 122.

3. Matthew Johnstone, *Quiet the Mind: An Illustrated Guide on How to Meditate*, London: Constable & Robinson, 2012, quoted in *The Times, times2,* 24 April 2012.

4. Katherine Weare, *Evidence for the Impact of Mindfulness on Children and Young People*, Exeter: Mood Disorders Centre, 2012, p. 2.

5. Dina Glouberman, *The Joy of Burnout*, p. 11.

PART THREE

Chapter 9

1. Bruce and Katherine Epperly, *Feed the Fire,* Cleveland, OH: Pilgrim Press, 2008, p. 102.

2. Dina Glouberman, *The Joy of Burnout*, p. 187.

Chapter 10

1. William Shakespeare, words uttered by Polonius in *Hamlet,* Act 1 Scene 3.

2. Kate Middleton, *Stress: How to De-stress Without Doing Less,* p. 75.

3. Julia Bueno, "Coaching – one of the fastest growing industries in the world" in *Therapy Today,* Vol. 21, Issue 7, September 2010, pp. 13–14.

Chapter 11

1. Donna Andronicos, *Coping with Burnout,* p. 61.

2. D.C. Khakha, "Caring for Carers: missing block in HIV/AIDS care", *The Nursing Journal of India,* Vol. 97, Issue 12, 2006, pp. 275–76.

Chapter 12
1. Survey by Harbour Salmon Company reported in *The Times* on 5 March 2013.

Chapter 13
1. Julia Cameron, *The Artist's Way: A Course in Discovering and Recovering Your Creative Self*, London: Pan Books, 1993, p. 166.

Chapter 14
1. Bruce and Katherine Epperly, *Feed the Fire*, Cleveland, OH: Pilgrim Press, 2008, p. 63.

Chapter 15
1. E. Ericson-Lidman and G. Strandberg, "Being closely connected to health care providers experiencing burnout: putting one's life on hold to help", *Journal of Family Nursing* 16 (1), 2010, pp. 101–123.